D0644629

Better English
Handle everyday situations
with confidence

Studymates

British History 1870–1918: The Emergence of a Nation
War: How War Became Global
Hitler and Nazi Germany: The Seduction of a Nation (3rd ed)
The English Reformation: The Effect on a Nation
European History 1870–1918: The Rise of Nationalism
Lenin, Stalin and Communist Russia: The Myth and Reality of
    Communism
Genetics: The Science of Genetics Revealed (2nd ed)
Organic Chemistry: How Organic Chemistry Works (2nd ed)
Chemistry: A's Chemistry Explained
Chemistry: Chemistry Calculations Explained
The New Science Teacher's Handbook
Mathematics for Adults: Basic Mathematics Explained
Calculus: How Calculus Works
Understanding Forces: How Forces Work
Algebra: Basic Algebra Explained
Plant Physiology: The Structure of Plants Explained
Poems to Live By
Shakespeare: The Barriers Removed
Chaucer: Approaching the Canterbury Tales
Poetry: The Secret Gems of Poetry Revealed
Better English: Handle Everyday Situations with Confidence
Better French: Become Fluent with Everyday Speech
Social Anthropology: Investigating Human Social Life
Statistics for Social Science: Data Handling Explained
Study Skills: Maximise Your Time to Pass Exams
Practical Drama and Theatre Arts: Practical Theatre Skills
    Explained
The War Poets 1914–18: The Secrets of Poems from the Great
    War
The Academic Essay: How to Plan, Draft, Write and Revise
Your Masters Thesis: How to Plan, Draft, Write and Revise
Your PhD Thesis: How to Plan, Draft, Write, Revise and Edit
    Your Thesis

Many other titles in preparation

Studymates
Helping You to Achieve

Better English
Handling everyday situations with confidence

Third edition

Dorothy Massey
BA(Eng) DipEd CertTESLA
Lecturer, Darlington College

www.studymates.co.uk

ISBN-10 1-84285-076-8
ISBN-13 978-1-84285-076-3

First edition 2000
Second edition 2003
Third edition 2005

This edition published by Studymates Limited,
Studymates House, Abergele, Conwy-County LL22 8DD,
United Kingdom.

Typeset by PDQ Typesetting, Newcastle-under-Lyme
Printed and Bound in the United Kingdom by the
Bell & Bain Ltd., Glasgow.

Contents

Preface

This is a course in everyday spoken English for adults whose mother tongue is not English. Students who are already able to read in English can use the book as a self-access guide. Students who have little or no reading skills, working with a class teacher or personal tutor can also use it.

ESOL students often find the formal English they learned in their home country is very different from that spoken by native English people. This course will encourage student autonomy by providing the language needed to meet everyday situations with confidence. The language, vocabulary and grammatical structures are authentic, but kept as simple as possible.

Each chapter covers one main topic, which is broken down into particular situations. All those topics most commonly requested are present, including health, education and job seeking. Topics requiring a more in-depth approach, such as English for driving or at work, have not been included.

I would like to thank the following for their valuable help and advice: Mr P. Donald, Mrs M. Donald, Mr & Mrs P Clough, Mr M. Sugden, Mrs J. Massey, Mrs P. Rossi, and Miss V. Nattrass. I would also like to thank my husband, Richard, for his patience and support.

Dorothy Massey

Talking About Yourself

In this chapter you will learn how to talk about yourself. You learn how to:

- talk about yourself – give your name, address, date of birth, say where you live and how long you've lived there, say where you come from, and whether you are married or single
- talk about your family – describe your parents, husband, children, and your extended family (grandparents, grandchildren, uncles, and aunts)
- talk about your job – say whether you are working, what you do, where you work, how long you have worked there, what you like or dislike about your work
- talk about your **hobbies** and **interests** – say which sports you play or watch, which musical **instruments** you play, and how to say what you like and don't like.

Talking about yourself

Language practice

What's your name?

My name is _____.

Where are you from? (Which country do you come from?)

I come from _____.

Where do you live?

I live in _____.

How long have you lived here?

I have lived here for _____ months/years.

Are you married?

> Yes, I am. Are you? *or*
>
> No, I'm single. What about you?

Real-life conversation

Scene: At a party

Shagufta:	Hi, I'm Shagufta.
Maria:	I'm Maria.
Shagufta:	Are you from Spain?
Maria:	No, I'm from Mexico. Where are you from?
Shagufta:	I'm from Pakistan.
Maria:	Do you live in Millbrook, Shagufta?
Shagufta:	Yes. Do you?
Maria:	Yes, I do.
Shagufta:	How long have you lived here?
Maria:	Two years now. What about you?
Shagufta:	Only three weeks. Do you like Millbrook?
Maria:	I love it. There's so much **going on**.
Shagufta:	Going on?
Maria:	Things to do. You know, **theatre, cinema, parties**.
Shagufta:	Ah, yes. I understand now.
Maria:	Are you married?
Shagufta:	Yes. That's my husband over there. What about you? Are you married?
Maria:	No. I'm young, free and single.

Talking about your family

Language practice

Do you have any children?

> No, I haven't any children. *or*
>
> Yes, I have a son/daughter. *or*
>
> Yes, I have _____children, _____boy(s) and _____ girl(s).

How old is he/she?
How old are they?
> He/she is _____ years/ months old.
> They are_____, _____, and _____.

Tip	• If a child is under two years old, we usually give the age in months, for example 'fifteen months'.

Real-life conversation
Scene: Lunchtime at work

Valerie:	**Have you got** any children, Anna?
Anna:	Yes, I've got three. Two boys and a girl.
Valerie:	Have you? How old are they?
Anna:	Hans is six, Karl is four and Heidi is only eighteen months. Have you got any children yourself?
Valerie:	Yeah, I've got two sons.
Anna:	And how old are they?
Valerie:	John Paul is eighteen and Dominique's twenty .. no, twenty-one.
Anna:	You can't have sons that age! How old are you?
Valerie:	Now that would be telling, wouldn't it?

Talking about your job

Language practice
Do you work? *or*
Are you employed/working?
> Yes. *or*
> No, I'm unemployed, I'm on the dole *or*
> No, I'm a **housewife**...No, I'm a **student**...

What do you do? OR
What's your job/occupation?
> I'm a _____.

Where do you work?
    I work at _____.

Who do you work for?
    I work for _____.

How long have you worked there?
    _____ months/years.

Real-life conversation

Scene: In the town centre

Mohammad: Ahmed. Haven't seen you for ages. How's
           things?
Ahmed: Fine. How's things with you?
Mohammed: Oh, not bad.
Ahmed: Are you working?
Mohammed: No, I'm still on the dole.

Ahmed: You're not, are you? I thought you got a
              job at Adams.
Mohammed: I did. I was made **redundant** in April.
Ahmed: Oh, Mohammed. I'm sorry to hear that.
Mohammed: That's okay. What about you? Are you
              employed?
Ahmed: Yes, I'm still working at the hospital.
Mohammed: That's good. How long have you worked
              there now?
Ahmed: Eight years.
Mohammed: Eight years. What's your job? Are you a
              doctor **or something?**
Ahmed: No, I'm a **porter.**
Mohammed: Oh. Do you like it?
Ahmed: Yes, I do. You work long hours you know,
              shifts, but the pay's not bad...and it's
              interesting. You meet some **strange** people.

Mohammed: I bet. There aren't any jobs going, are there?

Ahmed: Actually, there are. One of my **workmates** has just **retired**. Are you interested?

Mohammed: You bet I am.

Talking about your hobbies

Language practice

What are your hobbies? *or*

What do you do in your spare time?

I play_____. (sport)

I play the _____. (musical instrument)

Do/can you play (the) _____?

Yes, I do/can. Do/can you? *or*

No, I can't play _____.

Do you like (going to) the **cinema/theatre/opera**?

Yes, I do. *or*

No, not really.

Real-life situation

Scene: At a football match

John:	Ali. I didn't know you were a City **fan**.
Ali:	Yes. I love football. I'm **football mad**.
John:	Do you play?
Ali:	No. I love watching it, but I can't play. Can you?
John:	Yes. I play five-a-side.
Ali:	Five-a-side?
John:	Yes, you play indoors, five men to the team.
Ali:	Do you play anything else?
John:	I play cricket and I swim. Do you swim?
Ali:	No, but I play cricket.
John:	Will you be watching it on the **telly** tomorrow?
Ali:	No, I'm going to the theatre.

Language transfer

Going on (happening)

> *What's* **going on** over there?
> How long's this been **going on**?

Note – 'Going on' can also be a **phrasal verb**, for example:

> I am **going on** holiday tomorrow.
> We are **going on** an **outing** to the **zoo**.

Have you got . . .? (Do you have . . .?)

> **Have you got** any children?
> **Have you got** a pen I can **borrow**?

Have you got a car?
Have you got a light? (for a cigarette)

Or something (... used when you are not sure)
Are you a doctor **or something?**
Have you got a cold **or something?**
Would you like a coffee **or something?**

Football mad (... someone who likes football very much)
I'm football **mad.**
I'm **mad about** football.
Children are computer **mad.**

Also: to be mad on.
He's *mad on* cricket.
She's *mad on* **Kylie Minogue.**

Helping you learn

Progress questions

1. Give the following information about your family – their names (spelling if necessary), ages, dates of birth and jobs.

2. Make a list of questions you could ask someone about his or her job.

3. Do you have any **unusual** hobbies, or do you know someone who has?

Discussion points

1. Blood is thicker than water. (Family is more important than friends are.) Do you agree?

2. What do you like/dislike about your work?

3. Are British people sports mad?

Practical assignments

1 Practise giving your personal details to someone. Include your name, address and date of birth.

2 Ask someone about his or her work. Can you find out what they do, where they work, how long they've worked there and whether or not they like it?

3 Now ask someone about his or her hobbies. Do they play or watch any sports? Can they play any musical instruments? What kind of music do they like? Do they like cooking, dancing or going to the theatre?

Study tips

1 Learn to spell your name out loud. You will need to know the **alphabet**. If you don't know it ask an English speaker for help or buy a tape.

2 Use a dictionary to find out the names of more occupations and sports or hobbies. A photo dictionary is ideal.

Glossary

alphabet	the letters which make up a language (in English a, b, c etc.)
borrow	to get something which belongs to another person then give it back
cinema	a place where films (movies) are shown on a big screen
fan	short for fanatic, someone who likes something very much
hobbies	(*sing*. hobby) things you like to do when you are not at work
housewife	a woman who does not go to work, but looks after the house
illustrations	pictures, drawings or photographs
interests	see hobbies, things you do often and like

interesting	keeping your attention, making you want to know more
instrument	a tool, something you use. A musical instrument makes musical sounds.
Kylie Minogue	a popular singer
opera	drama or acting with music and songs
outing	a short journey or visit
parties	(*sing.* party) meetings of people to celebrate a birthday or special occasion
phrasal verb	a verb with a preposition, such as, to go on, take off, fall down
porter	the person in a hospital who helps move patients, laundry etc from one place to another
redundant	not needed, no longer having a job or occupation
retired	having left work, usually because of age or illness
shifts	times of work that are not the same every day, for example night shift or day shift. A split shift is two shifts in one day, for example, eight until twelve, then three until seven
strange	different, surprising
student	someone who is studying at school, college or university
telly	short for television. Example: Did you see the telly last night?
theatre	a place for plays and acting
unusual	see strange, different,
workmate	someone you work with
zoo	short for zoological garden, a place where wild animals are kept so that people can go and see them

Colloquial phrases

going on...	Why is that door closed? What's going on? (What's happening?)
have you got...?	Have you got a newspaper? (Do you have a newspaper?)
... or something	Have you got a newspaper, or magazine, or something?
mad about	I'm mad about the Kylie Minogue. (I like Kylie Minogue very much.)
mad on	I'm mad on cricket. (I like cricket very much.)

Social English

One-minute summary

In this chapter you will learn how to:

- make introductions – introduce yourself in a **formal/informal** way, introduce your family, friends, and colleagues
- say goodbye – learn different ways of saying goodbye, and practise other ways of taking leave or ending a conversation
- talk about the weather – identify different types of weather, comment on the weather, and talk about the weather **forecast**
- ask for help and information – ask for help from someone, ask if you can **borrow** something, ask for information in different situations
- deal with **invitations** – invite someone to your house, a party, or sports event, show interest and accept invitations, and say no without causing **offence**.

Making introductions

Language practice

Hello, I'm _____.
I'm _____. Pleased to meet you. *or*
I'm _____. It's (so) nice to meet you.
This is my husband/wife/sister.
Have you met _____?
He's/she's _____'s wife/husband etc.

Real-life conversation

Scene: A New Year party

Kang Tai:	Wei Li, have you met my husband?
Wei Li:	No, I don't think I have.
Kang Tai:	Would you like to meet him?
Wei Li:	Yes, of course.

Kang Tai:	Harry, come here, will you? This is Wei Li. Wei Li, this is my husband, Harry.
Wei Li:	It's nice to meet you at last. Kang Tai has told me so much about you.
Harry:	All good I hope.
Wei Li:	Of course. Oh, this is my husband, Ken. Ken, this is Kang Tai and her husband, Harry.
Harry:	Pleased to meet you. And who's this?
Ken:	This is our daughter, Polly.

Saying goodbye

Language practice

Goodbye. *or*
Cheerio. *or*
Bye.
See you later.
See you again some time.
(Well,) It was nice talking to you.
I must go now.
I have to go now.

Real-life conversation

Scene: Tomoko's house

Tomoko: **Would you like** another cup of tea?

Michiko: No thanks. I have to go now. I have to collect Mina from school.

Tomoko: What! Is it that time already? The afternoon has **flown by.**

Michiko: Yes. It has, hasn't it? I've really enjoyed it though.

Tomoko:	So have I. It's been nice talking to you.
Michiko:	Goodbye.
Tomoko:	Bye. See you next week.
Michiko:	See you.

Talking about the weather

Language practice

(What a) lovely/rotten/miserable day.   *or*
(What) lovely/rotten/miserable weather.
Yes, isn't it?

The forecast's bad/good.   *or*
The forecast said its going to get worse/better.

Real-life conversation

Scene: At a bus stop

Saljit:	Morning.
Nehab:	Not a very nice one, is it?
Saljit:	No. What miserable weather.
Nehab:	Rain again.
Saljit:	The forecast's good though.
Nehab:	Is it?

Saljit:	Yes. It's supposed to be sunny for the rest of the week.
Nehab:	That's good. **I'm sick of** rain.
Saljit:	So am I.

Asking for help or information

Language practice

Excuse me. Could you help me? *or*
Do you think you could give me a hand?
Could/can you **lend** me a/your_____? *or*
Could/can I **borrow** a/your_____?
Do you know where_____ is?
Do you know how to _____?
Do you know what to do?

Real-life conversation

Scene: on a train

Old woman:	Excuse me. Do you think you could give me a hand?
Young man:	Yes, of course. What can I do?
Old woman:	**It's my** suitcase. A young lady put it up there on the rack for me and I can't get it down.
Young man:	There you are.
Old woman:	Thank you. Thank you ever so much.
Young man:	It's a pleasure. Could I help you off the train?
Old woman:	Oh no. I'll manage now, thank you.

Making and receiving invitations

Language practice

Would you like to _____?

Yes, I'd love to.

When/where is it?

When will it start?

I'm afraid I can't, I'm busy that day/morning etc.

No, thank you I'm not keen on _____.

> **Tip**
> • If you **decline** an invitation it's polite to give a reason or excuse. It doesn't have to be true!

Real-life conversation:

Scene: After an English class

Monica:	We're having a party on Sunday. Would you like to come?
Maria:	A party? Yes, I'd love to. Where is it?
Monica:	At our house. At three oclock.
Maria:	Three. Oh, it's in the afternoon.
Monica:	Yes. It's a family party.
Maria:	Oh, I'm sorry. I'm afraid I can't come then. I **promised** the children I'd take them to the zoo.
Monica:	Oh well, another time maybe.

Language transfer

To be sick of...(tired of something, especially something you don't like)

I'm **sick of** rain.

I'm **sick of** these **horror** films, let's see a **comedy** instead.

I'm **sick of** telling you. Stop that now.

Would you like: used to offer something or to invite someone

Would you like a cup of tea?

Would you like more rice?

Would you like to come to our party?

Would you like to meet my husband?

It's my... (used to say what is wrong, to explain a problem or situation)

It's my suitcase. I can't reach it.

It's my daughter. She's ill.

It's my back. I have a back problem.

I'm afraid... (I'm sorry...)

    I'm afraid I can't come then.

    I'm afraid there's only one left.

    I'm afraid we only have coffee, will that do?

- *Note:* to be afraid can also mean to have fear or be scared.

Helping you learn

Progress questions

1 Can you think of three things that you might say when you are introduced to someone?

2 How many greetings can you think of:
(a) in English?
(b) in your language?

3 And how many ways can you think of saying goodbye?

Discussion points

1 Why are British people always talking about the weather?

2 British weather is unpredictable (always changing). What was the weather like in your home country?

3 Do you find it easy or difficult to decline invitations? What excuses do you use?

Practical assignments

1 Introduce yourself to someone you don't know.

2 Invite somebody to your house, or invite him or her to your English class, a club, theatre or sporting event.

3 Ask a stranger for information. Some examples might be to ask:
(a) The opening hours of the library, swimming pool etc.
(b) How to get a bus to another town, city or village.
(c) Where you can buy something you want (food, clothing, etc.)

Study tips

1 Learn the vocabulary for family relationships. Why not make your own family tree or a list of your family's names with their relationship to you. Remember the difficult ones such as in-laws, nephews, nieces and cousins.
– Your mother's parents are your maternal grandparents.
– Your father's parents are your paternal grandparents.

2 Practise asking to borrow things, for example, 'Do you have a pencil?'

Glossary

borrow	to get something which belongs to another person, then give it back
comedy	film, book or play that makes you laugh
decline	to say 'no' to
forecast	what you think will happen, for example weather forecast, cricket forecast, news forecast
formal	used for a special or important time or person
horror	a film, book or play that frightens you
informal	used with friends or family
invitation	an offer to come somewhere, or to do something
lend	to give something to somebody, then get it back
miserable	unhappy. Miserable weather is cold, wet or foggy weather.
offence	something that makes someone upset or angry
promise	to say that you will do something
rotten	nasty, bad (see miserable)

Colloquial phrases

fly by, flown by. . .	The week has flown by! (The week has passed very quickly.) We had a great holiday. The time flew by.
I'm afraid . . .	I'm afraid I forgot. (I'm sorry, I forgot.) I'm afraid I can't do that. I'm afraid I don't agree.
I'm sick of . . .	I'm sick of studying. (I'm tired of studying. I'm fed up with studying.)
It's my . . .	It's my passport. (I have a problem with my passport.) It's my sister. She won't agree to go. It's my boss. He makes me work too hard.
Would you like . . .	Would you like a cup of tea? (Do you want a cup of tea?) Would you like to see a film?

Getting About

In this chapter you will learn how to:

■ ask for directions – ask how to get to a **specific** bank or hotel, and ask how to get to the nearest bank or hotel

■ give directions – learn the vocabulary needed to give directions, give directions to your house, and give directions to people on foot or travelling by car

■ use public transport – find out where and when a bus/train leaves, take a taxi, and buy train tickets (including cheap deals)

■ book a holiday – ask for information on holidays, book accommodation and flights, and ask about payment.

Asking for directions

Language practice

Excuse me, can you tell me the way to _____?

Excuse me, can you tell me where the nearest _____ is?

Excuse me, where's the nearest _____?

Excuse me, is there a _____ nearby?

Is this the way to _____?

I'm trying to get to _____.

Real-life conversation

Mario: Excuse me, can you tell me the way to the nearest bank?

Stranger: Yes, there's one along the street on the left-hand side.

Mario: Does it have a **cash dispenser**?

Stranger: No, I don't think it does.

Mario: Is there a bank nearby which does?

Stranger: Theres a few in the High Street with **cashpoints**.

Mario: Is that the High Street up there?

Stranger: Yes. That's it.

Mario: Thank you.

Stranger: You're welcome.

Giving directions

Language practice

It's on the left/right.

It's opposite the _____. It's facing the _____.

It's next to_____. It's beside _____.

Turn left at the **roundabout**.

Turn right at the **junction/crossroads**.

Go straight on/over/ahead at the roundabout.
Take the first/second/third right/left.

Real-life conversation

Scene: Mr Adam's home
The telephone rings. Mr Adams answers it.

Mr Adams: Hello. Millbrook 658951.

Mr Singh: Hello. Is that Mr Adams?

Mr Adams: Yes, speaking. Can I help you?

Mr Singh: Oh. Hello. Mr Adams. It's Mr Singh here. Gita's father. Gita's got an invitation to your son's party.

Mr Adams: Ah, yes. His birthday party on Saturday.

Mr Singh: Yes. Gita would like to come, but I don't know how to get to your house.

Mr Adams: I see. Where are you coming from?

Mr Singh: We live in Eastbrook. In the new housing estate, near the golf course.

Mr Adams: Okay. Do you know how to get to Millbrook?

Mr Singh: Yes, but I've only been to the main street where the post office is.

Mr Adams:	Do you know where the library is?
Mr Singh:	No.
Mr Adams:	Well, if you carry on up the main street past the post office you'll see the library on the right. It's an old building. Used to be the primary school. Turn left at the library and left again into Primrose Hill. Go straight up Primrose Hill until you see the church. Turn left at the next junction into Tennyson Court.
Mr Singh:	What was that?
Mr Adams:	Left into Tennyson Court. Tennyson. T-E-N-N-Y-S-O-N.
Mr Singh:	Thank you.
Mr Adams:	Then take the second right into Wordsworth, W-O-
Mr Singh:	Yes. I know Wordsworth Drive.
Mr Adams:	Yes. Keats Drive is the first left. Our house is the third on the right. We have a red garage door.
Mr Singh:	Oh, thank you, Mr Adams. Those were excellent directions. I'm sure we'll find your house now.
Mr Adams:	I hope so. I'll see you on Saturday then,
Mr Singh:	Yes, see you then. Goodbye.
Mr Adams:	Bye.

Using public transport

Language practice

What time's the next bus/train/tube to _____?
Where does the bus/train/tube leave?
Where can I get a bus/train to _____.
Do you go to_____? *or*
Can you take me to _____?
How much is it to _____?
I'd like a single/(day) return to _____, please.
I'd like to buy a Family/Student **railcard**/ bus pass.

<table>
<tr><td>**Tip**</td><td>● If you travel **regularly** you might be able to save money by buying a railcard, **bus pass** or weekly ticket.</td></tr>
</table>

Real-life situation

Scene: At the train station ticket office

Carlos: Hello. I'd like a ticket to London, please.
Attendant: Single or return?
Carlos: Return, please.
Attendant: Are you leaving today?

Carlos:	Yes. I'd like to catch the next train if I can. When does it leave?
Attendant:	The next one's at 10.13. Change at York.
Carlos:	It's not an **express** then? What time will it get to London?
Attendant:	It arrives in Kings Cross at 14.12.
Carlos:	Oh. That's fine.
Attendant:	When are you planning to return, sir?
Carlos:	On Friday.
Attendant:	This Friday?
Carlos:	Yes.
Attendant:	That's okay. Your ticket's **valid** for a month.
Carlos:	Where does the train leave?
Attendant:	Platform One. Over the bridge.
Carlos:	Thank you.

Booking a holiday

Language practice

Can I take some brochures for Spain/Italy etc?   *or*
Do you have any brochures for Germany?
I'd like to book a single/double/twin/family room in the
_____for nights/from the_____ th to the
_____th **inclusive**.

How much would that be?

Do you need a **deposit**?

When do I pay the **balance**?

Could you **suggest** an **alternative** hotel in the same area? In the same price **range**?

I'd like to book a flight/holiday to _____.

Real-life conversation

Scene: A travel agency

Assistant:	Good morning. How can I help you?
Fauzia:	My family wants to go to Malta at Easter.
Assistant:	I see. Have you seen our brochures on Malta?
Fauzia:	No. We just decided yesterday. My husband asked me to book it.
Assistant:	Well, a few companies do packages to Malta, but Easter is a very busy time. I'll see what I can do. There's one here leaving on Thursday the 17th. Flight from Teeside. Return the following Thursday.
Fauzia:	My husband has to go back to work on the Thursday. Do you have anything shorter?
Assistant:	We might have one, but you'd have to fly from Newcastle. Here we are. Leave Thursday 17th at 6.15 return Tuesday 22nd at 17.00.
Fauzia:	That sounds great!

Language transfer

Carry on (continue)

> **Carry on** up the street.
>
> **Carry on** straight-ahead at the next roundabout.
>
> **Carry on** like that and you will be ill.

● *Note:* A 'carry on' can also mean a disturbance, a commotion, or something annoying. 'Did you see that fight in the street? What a **carry on**!'

Used to be (when the nature of something or someone has changed)

> The library **used to be** a school.
> He's a teacher now, but he **used to be** a doctor.
> The garden **used to be** so pretty, but now it's overgrown and untidy.

Helping you learn

Progress questions

1 How many situations can you think of where you might say, 'Excuse me'? What is the equivalent in your language?

2 How many methods of payment can you think of? Which do you use?

3 A 'landmark' is a well-known building or monument. Landmarks are useful when giving directions. Suggest some local landmarks when giving directions to your home, or college.

Practical assignments

1 Give someone directions to your house from a local landmark or place you know well. Remember to ask whether they are going by car or on foot.

2 Go into a town or city centre and ask for directions to a well-known building, such as a hotel or station. Did you understand the directions?

1 If you travel by bus or train ask about special offers or railcards. You might like to ask for leaflets on some of the following:

Family Railcards
Senior Railcards (age 60+)
Young Persons Railcard (16–25)
Discounts for Group Travel

Some stations may have leaflets on scenic rail routes, tourist attractions and walks.

2 Ask your local travel agent for some holiday brochures and practise booking holidays.

Discussion points

3 People have different ways of giving directions. For example, some people say, 'First left, second right' and so on. Others use street names or local landmarks, for example 'Past the library, there's a police station on the left.' Which do you prefer?

1 Which methods of public transport do you use most often – bus, train, taxi or the underground? Which do you prefer and why?

2 Do you like package holidays, or do you book your travel and accommodation separately? What are the advantages and disadvantages of these options?

Study tips

3 Buy or borrow street or road maps of your local area. Practise giving directions from one place to another.

4 If you are booking a holiday, prepare by thinking about what information the travel agent will need to know. The agent will need to know where you want to go, who is going with you, when you want to go, and other details.

Glossary

accommodation   a place to stay, hotel, guest house etc.

alternative	another, a different one
balance	amount still to be paid
bus pass	a card that gives you cheap or free bus travel
cash dispenser	a machine that lets you take cash from a bank
cashpoint	a place with a cash dispenser
crossroads	the place where two roads cross
deposit	the first payment for something
express	very fast
inclusive	where the first and last dates are part of the total, for example from 10th to 13th inclusive is 4 days
junction	a place where roads meet
railcard	a card that gives you cheap rail travel
range	in the same price range means 'of about the same price'
roundabout	a junction where roads meet in a circle
specific	a special or important thing or place
suggest	give an example of, to tell someone
valid	able to be used (not out of date)

Colloquial phrases

carry on . . .	Let's carry on walking. (Let's continue walking. Let's go on walking.)
	Let's carry on with what we were doing.
	I'm tired, I can't carry on.
	What a carry on! (What a disturbance!)
	Stop carrying on!
used to be . . .	This hotel used to be cheap. (In the past, this hotel was cheap.)
	The food used to be good.
	He used to be very shy.
	It's not like it used to be.
	Things aren't what they used to be.

4 Shopping

One-minute summary

In this chapter you will learn how to:

■ ask the assistant for help − ask to see something you might like to buy, and say you don't need help

■ buy clothing and shoes − ask to try things on, get the right size, ask about payment methods

■ return faulty goods − describe the fault, and ask for an exchange or refund

■ make a complaint − complain about a fault, complain about bad service, ask to see the manager or someone in charge, and say that you are not satisfied or happy.

Asking for help

Language practice

Could you show me that/those _____ please?

Could I see that/those _____?

I'd like to buy a/some _____.

I'm just looking,

I like the green one.

Real-life conversation

Scene: At the jeweller's

Assistant:	Good morning. Can I help you?
Martina:	We'd like to look at some **engagement** rings, please.
Assistant:	I see. Are you looking for any **particular type**?
Martina:	I've seen a few I like in the window. Could we see them, please?
Assistant:	Of course. Do you know which **tray** they are on?
Martina:	Yes. Numbers 32 and 34.

Assistant:	That's the **sapphire** ones. There you are. Which one's do you like?
Martina:	I like this one, this one here... oh, and that one there.
Assistant:	Would you like to try them on?
Martina:	Yes, please.

Buying clothes and shoes

Language practice

Could I try this/these on?

Where's the changing room?

I don't know my size, could you **measure** me?

Do you have a **top** to **match** this skirt?

Do you have this in a [size] 10/12 etc?

Do you have this in another colour?

It's/they are too big/small/short/long/tight.

Does it **suit** me?

It doesn't suit me.

They don't suit me.

I don't like the **style**/colour/sleeves etc.

- *Note*: 'this' shirt/dress/coat, but
      'these' shoes/trousers/shorts/pyjamas

Do you take a cheque/**credit/debit** cards?
Can I pay by Visa/MasterCard?

Real-life conversation

Scene: a high street store

Ester:	Excuse me. Can I try these on?
Assistant:	Yes, of course. How many **items** do you have?
Ester:	Four.
Assistant:	Follow me. That **cubicle**'s free. Shout if you **need a hand**.
Ester:	Excuse me. I like the jacket, but the skirt's too big.
Assistant:	What size have you got? A fourteen. Would you like to try it in a twelve?
Ester:	Yes, please.
Assistant:	What about the blouse?
Ester:	I'm not sure whether I like it, actually.
Assistant:	Do you want white?
Ester:	No. Not **particularly**. I just want something to go with the **suit**.
Assistant:	Would you like me to see if I can find anything for you?
Ester:	Oh, yes, please.
Assistant:	Here's the skirt in a twelve and **a couple of** blouses.
Ester:	Thank you...
Assistant:	...How did you get on?
Ester:	The skirt fits in a twelve. I'll take the skirt and jacket and this cream blouse. Oh, and I need a pair of shoes.
Assistant:	What size are you?
Ester:	A five, sometimes a five and a half.

Assistant:	Shoes or sandals?
Ester:	Hmm. Sandals might be nice.
Assistant:	We have some lovely cream ones here.
Ester:	No. They're too high. I like a lower heel.
Assistant:	What about these?
Ester:	They're better. I'll try them on.
Assistant:	We don't have them in half sizes. I'll get you them in a five.
Ester:	Thanks.
Ester:	I'll take these. Can I pay by cheque?
Assistant:	Yes, If you have a cheque guarantee **card**.

Returning goods

Language practice

I'd like to return this/these.
I bought it/them here yesterday/last week/last month.
The **zip** is broken.
The **hem** has come down.
The colour has **run**.
It's **shrunk**.
It doesn't work properly.
It's **scratched/dented/**broken.
There's a part missing.
It's no good to me.

Real-life conversation

Scene: a clothes shop

Assistant:	Hello. Can I help you?
Shima:	Yes. I hope so. I want to return this dress.
Assistant:	Oh. Is there something wrong with it?
Shima:	The first time I washed it, the colour ran and it shrank.
Assistant:	Did you follow the washing instructions?
Shima:	Yes. Of course I did.
Assistant:	Do you have your receipt?

Shima:	Yes. Here it is. I bought it in your Oxford **branch** last week.
Assistant:	That's okay. Do you want to **exchange** it, or would you like a **refund**?
Shima:	**I'd rather have** a refund, please.
Assistant:	Certainly, madam. (*Gives money.*) There you are.

Making a complaint

Language practice

I'd like to see the manager, please.
I want to make a complaint.
I'm not happy with the iron/washing machine etc. I bought here.
I'm sorry, but I'm not prepared to **accept** that.

Real-life conversation

Scene: an electrical goods shop

Assistant:	Good morning, Sir. How may I help you?
Ivan:	I'd like to see the manager, please.
Assistant:	I'm afraid the manager's not in today. Can I help?
Ivan:	I want to make a complaint about my washing machine.
Assistant:	Oh. I see. What's wrong with it?
Ivan:	It's broken down again. I would like a new one.
Assistant:	When did you buy it?
Ivan:	Two months ago.
Assistant:	Do you have the receipt?
Ivan:	Yes, I have it here. And the repair notes. This is the third time it's broken down. We have four children, so we need a machine that works.
Assistant:	I'll phone our office . . .

Assistant:	...They say they can come and look at it on Friday. If it can't be repaired they will get you a replacement.
Ivan:	Im sorry, I'm not prepared to accept that. That's no good to me. I want a new machine. Who's in charge here?
Assistant:	The supervisor, but...
Ivan:	I'd like to speak to him.
Supervisor:	Yes, sir. Can I help you?
Ivan:	Yes. The washing machine I bought has broken down again. It's the third time. Your assistant says someone will come to repair it on Friday, but I want a new machine.
Supervisor:	Did you say the third time? How long have you had it?
Ivan:	Less than two months.
Supervisor:	Oh. I'll phone and get you a replacement.
Ivan:	Could you get it as soon as possible?
Supervisor:	I'll see what I can do...
Supervisor:	...Tomorrow?
Ivan:	Oh, yes. That's great. Thank you ever so much.

Language transfer

A couple of (two)
Here's **a couple of** blouses.
He'll be here in **a couple of** minutes.
There's **a couple of** strange men outside my house.

I'd rather... I would prefer... (used to express your opinion to a suggestion)
I'd rather have a refund please.
I don't drink coffee; **I'd rather** have tea.
I'd rather go to a football match than watch it on television.

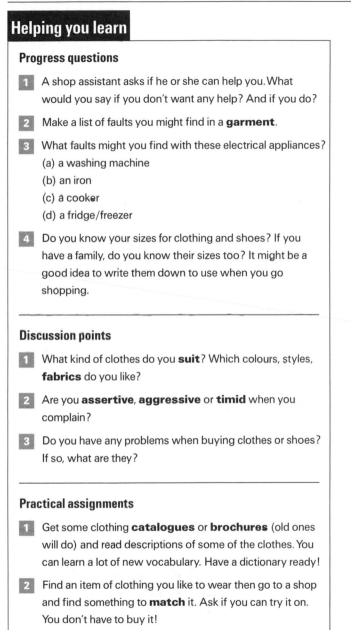

Helping you learn

Progress questions

1 A shop assistant asks if he or she can help you. What would you say if you don't want any help? And if you do?

2 Make a list of faults you might find in a **garment**.

3 What faults might you find with these electrical appliances?
(a) a washing machine
(b) an iron
(c) a cooker
(d) a fridge/freezer

4 Do you know your sizes for clothing and shoes? If you have a family, do you know their sizes too? It might be a good idea to write them down to use when you go shopping.

Discussion points

1 What kind of clothes do you **suit**? Which colours, styles, **fabrics** do you like?

2 Are you **assertive**, **aggressive** or **timid** when you complain?

3 Do you have any problems when buying clothes or shoes? If so, what are they?

Practical assignments

1 Get some clothing **catalogues** or **brochures** (old ones will do) and read descriptions of some of the clothes. You can learn a lot of new vocabulary. Have a dictionary ready!

2 Find an item of clothing you like to wear then go to a shop and find something to **match** it. Ask if you can try it on. You don't have to buy it!

3 With a friend, relative or teacher, practise returning goods and making complaints. Be assertive!

Glossary

assertive	saying what you want to in a confident way
aggressive	being rude or getting angry or nasty
branch	one of a group or chain of shops, banks or restaurants
brochures	small books to advertise something
catalogues	books from which you can order things you want to buy
credit card	a card that lets you buy things and pay for them later
cubicle	a small room usually used for changing your clothes
debit card	a card that you use instead of cash: the money is taken from your bank account
engagement	promise of marriage
exchange	to change for something else
fabrics	types of material used for clothes, for example wool, cotton, silk
hem	the edge of a piece of clothing that has been sewn
item	a thing
match	go well together or is the same as
measure	to find
particular(ly)	special
receipt	a piece of paper you get when you pay for something
run	colours mixing together when something is washed
sapphire	a blue stone used in jewellery
shrunk	the past tense of the verb to shrink, to get smaller
style	the fashion or design of something
suit, a	a suit, jacket with trousers or a skirt to match
suit, to	to suit something, to look good in something. 'That dress suits you.'
timid	frightened, nervous, shy

top	a piece of clothing worn on the top half of the body, usually with short sleeves or no sleeves at all
tray	something on which jewellery is displayed or food is served
type	a kind of
zip	(American, zipper) a fastener with small teeth that fit together

Colloquial phrases

a couple of	a couple of minutes. (Two minutes.)
I'd rather...	I'd rather go home. I would prefer to go home, rather than stay here.
need a hand	I need a hand with this bag. (Please help me with this bag.)
	I need someone to give me a hand.

Going to the Doctor's

Making an appointment

Language practice

Hello, I'd like to make an appointment (for my son, for my husband) please.

My/his/her date of birth is _____.

I'm sorry, that's not suitable. Can you give me another appointment, please?

I can't come then.

Yes, that's fine, thank you.

Real-life conversation

Scene: The doctor's surgery

Receptionist: Good morning, can I help you?

Fareha: Yes. I want to make an appointment to see the doctor.
Receptionist: Who's your doctor?
Fareha: **Dr** Chatterjee.
Receptionist: Dr Chatterjee's fully **booked** this week. I could give you Dr Brown on Thursday at 9.
Fareha: Is that a woman doctor?
Receptionist: No, it's a man. Do you want a female doctor?
Fareha: Yes, please.
Receptionist: There's one with Dr Smith on Friday at 9.45.
Fareha: I'm sorry. I can't come on Friday morning,
Receptionist: Well, it's going to be next week then, I'm **afraid**. Monday the 14th at five to five. That's with Dr Chatterjee.
Fareha: Yes, that will be fine.
Receptionist: What's the name?
Fareha: Fareha Hassif.
Receptionist: Can you spell it?
Fareha: Hassif, H-A-S-S-I-F. Fareha, F-A-R-E-H-A.
Receptionist: And your date of birth?
Fareha: Seven, eight, sixty-two.
Receptionist: Okay, so that's Monday the fourteenth at five to five.
Fareha: Monday at 4.55. Thank you. Bye.

Saying what's wrong

Language practice

I've got a headache.

I've got a **sore** throat.

I've had it since Monday/since last week/since last month.

I've **been getting** a lot of headaches.

I've **been getting** a lot of stomach pains recently.

I've been getting them for_____ weeks/for
_____ days.

I've been feeling very tired/sick/**dizzy**.

I think I've broken my leg/arm/wrist.

Real-life conversation

Scene: the doctor's surgery

Fareha: Hello.

Doctor: Hello. Mrs Hassif, isn't it?

Fareha: Yes.

Doctor: And how can I help you today?

Fareha: Well, I haven't been feeling well lately.

Doctor: Oh dear, I'm sorry to hear that. What's
            wrong?

Fareha: I feel tired all the time and I've been
            getting a lot of headaches.

Doctor: I see. Have you been sleeping well?

Fareha: Yes, but I still feel tired.

Doctor: Do you get plenty of exercise and fresh air?

Fareha: Yes. I walk everywhere and I go swimming.

Doctor: Have you had any sickness or dizziness?

Fareha: No sickness, but sometimes I go dizzy.
            Yesterday, when I went upstairs, I felt
            dizzy. I thought I was going to **faint**.

Doctor: I see.

Understanding the doctor's instructions

Language practice

- *Note* – The doctor might say the following, not the patient. Make sure you understand the instructions, so that you will know what to do.

I'm going to examine your chest/eyes/throat etc.
I'm going to take your blood **pressure**.
I'll need to take a blood sample. Can you **roll up** your sleeve?
Can you take off your coat/jumper?
You'll need to go for an **X-ray**.
I'll give you a prescription for some **pain-killers/antibiotics**.
Take one twice a day.
Take two once a day
Take two three times a day.
Dissolve them in water.

Real-life conversation

Scene: at the doctor's surgery

Doctor: I'm going to take your **blood pressure**.
           Could you take your coat off, please?
Fareha: Would you like me to take my jumper off too?
Doctor: No, can you just roll up your sleeve? Good. Your blood pressure's fine.
Fareha: That's good.
Doctor: Yes. I'd like a sample of your blood and urine too. Heres a bottle for a urine sample. Can you hand it in as soon as possible?
Fareha: Yes. I'll bring it in tomorrow.

Doctor: Thank you. Now, I'll need some blood. Could you roll up your sleeve again? That **looks like** a good **vein** there. That's it. Press that cotton wool on for a while to stop the bleeding. There's a plaster for you.

Asking questions

Language practice

How many tablets do I take each day?
When do I take the tablets/medicine?
When will I get the results of this test?
How will I get the results of this test?
Will I need to see a **specialist**?
Is it serious?

I don't understand. Could you write it down, please?

Real-life conversation

Scene: at the doctor's surgery

Fareha: When will I get the results of these tests?
Doctor: They usually take a few days.
Fareha: Do I need to telephone the surgery?
Doctor: No. We will phone you when the results come back. Then I'd like you to make another appointment to see me.
Fareha: Why are you taking these tests? What do you think is wrong with me?
Doctor: I think you might be **anaemic**.
Fareha: Anaemic? What does that mean?
Doctor: You might not have enough iron in your blood.
Fareha: Iron... Ironing? I don't understand. Could you write it down, please?
Doctor: Iron?
Fareha: Yes and an... an...

Doctor:	Anaemic?
Fareha:	Yes.
Doctor:	There you are.
Fareha:	Thank you. I'll look it up in my dictionary. Is it serious?
Doctor:	No. Hopefully you'll just need some tablets and you'll be fine again.
Fareha:	Oh good.
Doctor:	Do you have any more questions?
Fareha:	No, I don't think so.

Language transfer

Been getting (used for something you have got or had recently)

I've **been getting** a lot of headaches.
I've **been getting** my hair done (*cut or styled at the hairdresser's*).
John's **been getting** a new car.

To look like (to appear to be, to resemble)
That **looks like** a good vein.
It **looks like** (its going to) snow.
Is that your daughter? She **looks like** you.

Helping you learn

Progress questions

1 What information will the receptionist need when you make an appointment to see the doctor?

2 When do you use 'for' and when do you use 'since'?

3 The following words might be found on medicines or tablets. What do they mean? Use a dictionary to help you: chew, swallow, dissolve, **linctus**, soluble, capsule, **lozenge**.

Discussion points

1 Do you think it is useful to learn First Aid (quick help that people give an **injured** person before the doctor comes)? Give reasons for your answer.

2 What do you think of the health service in Britain? Compare it with that in your home country.

Practical assignments

1 If you haven't got one already, buy or make a first aid kit. Ask for advice at your local **pharmacy** if you don't know what to include.

2 Practise making appointments with a friend or teacher. Remember to practise making appointments for other members of your family and asking to change the date or time of your appointments.

Study tips

1 Make a list of common illnesses. Use a dictionary to help you. What are the symptoms of these illnesses?

2 Giving times in English is difficult, for example, 9.50 is ten to ten. If you don't feel confident about giving and/or understanding times in English, practise.

3 If you need to make an appointment by telephone, make sure you have a pen and paper. Before you phone write down your name, address and date of birth or those of the person for whom you are making the appointment. Practise giving them clearly. When you are given an appointment, write down the time and date and check it.

Glossary

afraid	sorry
alternative	another one, a different or new one
anaemic	not having enough red blood cells in the blood. Anaemia is caused by not having enough **iron** in the body.
antibiotics	tablets or medicines that fight infection. Penicillin is an antibiotic.
blood pressure	the amount of pressure the heart is working under to feed oxygen to the body. The reading taken by the doctor has two figures. The top figure shows the heart in its working period the second in its resting period.
booked	fully booked, to have no appointments or vacancies left
dizzy	unsteady, having a strange feeling in your head, which sometimes makes you fall down. Dizziness is the feeling you get when you go round and round quickly.
Dr	short for doctor
duration	the time something lasts
faint	to fall and become unconscious (see glossary, chapter 10) for a short time
injured	hurt, having cuts, wounds, or broken bones
iron	a mineral found in red meat and green vegetables, which is needed to keep blood healthy
linctus	a thick, syrup-like cough medicine
lozenge	a rectangular tablet that you suck to help a sore throat

medication	tablets and medicines
painkillers	tablets to take away pain, such as aspirin and paracetamol
pharmacy	chemist shop, shop where you buy medicines
specialist	an expert in one particular area of a subject (in this case medicine)
vein	a thin, blue tube through which blood passes round the body
worrying	making you afraid that something bad might be happening or about to happen
x-ray	a photograph of your bones

Colloquial phrases

been getting . . .	I've been getting much stronger this week. I've been getting out more.
looks like . . .	It looks like she has to go into hospital. It looks like something serious.

6 At School

One-minute summary

In this chapter you will learn how to:

- **register** your child for school – ask how to register your child, answer questions about your child, and ask questions
- tell the teacher about – your child's health, diet, **behaviour, customs, culture** or religion
- ask the teacher about – your child's behaviour, your child's **progress**
- make the most of parent evenings – ask suitable questions, and talk about any **worries** or problems.

Registering your child for school

Language practice

I'd like to register my son/daughter for school please.
My name is _____.
Our address is _____.
His/her date of birth is _____.
He/she goes to _____ nursery/school.
When will he/she start school?

Real-life conversation

Scene: an infant school

Nurinder: Hello, I'd like to register my son here, please.

Secretary: Yes, of course. Could you fill in this form?

Nurinder: Yes. There you are.

Secretary: You haven't put on his date of birth.

Nurinder: Oh. Sorry. I missed that. It's the fifth of July.

Secretary: The fifth of July?

Nurinder: Yes.

Secretary: Is he at nursery school?

Nurinder: Yes. He goes to Millbank Nursery.

Secretary: Okay, that's fine. I'll put his name on the list and we'll contact you nearer the time.

Nurinder: When will he start school?

Secretary: The September after his fourth birthday.

Nurinder: So you'll send me a letter?

Secretary: Yes.

Nurinder: What are school hours?

Secretary: Normal school hours are nine to three thirty, but when he starts he will come mornings only for a week, then afternoons for a week. Would you like to see round the school?

Nurinder: Oh, yes please.

Telling the teacher about your child

Language practice

I'd like to see _____'s teacher, please.

_____ is a **vegetarian**.

_____ is a **Muslim**. He/she only eats halal meat.

_____is **allergic** to _____.

He can't eat anything containing it.

She can't eat drink anything containing them.

_____ can't come to school tomorrow morning/ afternoon because he/she is going to the doctor's/going to the dentist's.

_____couldn't come to school yesterday because he/ she was ill.

He/she will be off school for a week/for a fortnight/for a few days.

He/she has **flu, mumps, measles.**

I'd like to discuss his/her school report.

Real-life conversation

Scene: the infant school

Maria:	I'd like to see Sandra's teacher, please.
Secretary:	Sandra Moretti? She's in the **reception** class, isn't she?
Maria:	Yes, that's right.
Secretary:	Her teacher is Mrs Green. Do you know how to get to the classroom?
Maria:	Yes, thanks...
Maria:	Mrs Green, I'm Maria Moretti, Sandra's mother.
Mrs Green:	Oh, Mrs Moretti. I'm pleased to meet you. Sandra is **settling in** well. She was a little shy at first, but she seems happy now.
Maria:	That's good. There are a few things I must tell you about Maria. She is a vegetarian, but I would like her to have school dinners.
Mrs Green:	That's okay. The school provides a good range of vegetarian food.
Maria:	Good. She is also allergic to nuts. She mustn't eat anything at all with nuts in.
Mrs Green:	I see. I'll make sure that all the catering staff is aware of that. Is there anything else I should know?

Maria: Yes. She can't come to school tomorrow morning because she has to go to the dentist.

Asking the teacher for information

Language practice

How is _____ getting on?
How much dinner money does he/she need?

How and when do I pay her dinner money?
When is the mid-term break?
How do I join the PTA (Parent Teacher Association)?
Will he/she have any school health checks this year/term?

Real-life conversation

Scene: at junior school

Miyuki: Hello, Mr Rossi. Could I speak to you for a minute?
Mr Rossi: Yes, of course. Is it about Mia?

Miyuki:	Yes. I was wondering how she is getting on.
Mr Rossi:	She's doing well. I think she's finding it difficult to understand me sometimes, but she's coping well.
Miyuki:	She seems quite happy.
Mr Rossi:	Oh yes, she is enjoying it very much.
Miyuki:	I have a few questions to ask you.
Mr Rossi:	Yes, of course.
Miyuki:	I'd like to join the PTA. How do I do that?
Mr Rossi:	You can just go along to the next meeting and join then. If you ask the secretary she'll tell you when the next meeting is.
Miyuki:	I see. Thank you. Also, when is the mid-term break?
Mr Rossi:	From the 8th to the 12th of February.
Miyuki:	Thank you.
Mr Rossi:	Was there anything else?
Miyuki:	Yes. Now what was it? Ah, yes, I remember. Will Mia have any school health checks this year?
Mr Rossi:	Yes. She will have a **medical**. The doctor will check her general health, including her sight and hearing.
Miyuki:	That's good. Thank you.

Making the most of parents evenings

Language practice

Can you tell me where to find _____?

I'm Mr/Mrs _____, _____'s mother/father.

How is _____ **getting on**?

What can I do to help him/her at home?

Does he/she pay **attention** in class?

Are there any **subjects** he/she finds particularly difficult?

Is there anything I/we should know about?

Real-life conversation

Scene: Mr Brown's classroom

Mr Patel: Hello, Mr Brown. I'm Gita Patel's father.

Mr Brown: Mr Patel. Pleased to meet you.

Mr Patel: Pleased to meet you too. How is Gita getting on?

Mr Brown: She's done very well this year. She's made very good progress with her reading.

Mr Patel: I've been helping her with it at home. She likes reading. Are there any subjects she finds difficult?

Mr Brown: Yes. She's struggling with History. I don't think she's interested in it.

Mr Patel: I'm afraid I didn't like History either. Is there anything I can do to help her at home?

Mr Brown: Well, she likes reading. Perhaps you could buy some books on historical **topics** or borrow some from the library.

Mr Patel: Yes. I'll do that. You never know, I might find them interesting too. Does Gita work well?

Mr Brown: Yes, most of the time.

Mr Patel: And is she well behaved?

Mr Brown: Oh yes, she's a very good girl.

Mr Patel: That's good. **I'm pleased to** hear that.

Language transfer

Getting on (doing well, progressing)

I was wondering how she's **getting on**.
How's she **getting on** with History?
Sarah is **getting on** well with her new mother-in-law.

- *Note*: 'Getting on' (or 'getting on a bit') can also mean getting old.

How's your father? He must be **getting on** now.
That horse ran well. It must be **getting on a bit,** you know.

I'm pleased to (it's a pleasure.../ it's very good to...)
I'm **pleased to** hear that.
I'm **pleased to** meet you.

- *Note* – 'I'm pleased to see' means to be happy or glad that something has happened.

I'm **pleased to see** you took my advice.
I'm **pleased to see** you're better now.

Helping you learn

Progress questions

1 What information are you asked for when you register a child for school or nursery?

2 What questions might you like to ask?

3 What would you expect to talk about at a school parents' evening?

Discussion points

1 Parents should form a good relationship with their child or children's teacher/s.

2 Education is the **role** of the parent, teacher or both? How much do you think parents should be responsible for educating their children?

3 Do you think that education today is better or worse than when you went to school yourself?

Practical assignments

1 Ask a teacher how your child is getting on at school or nursery. You might like to ask about his or her behaviour, **strengths**, **weaknesses**, relationships with other children and teachers.

2 Practise a parents' evening with a friend, relative or teacher.

3 Find out which societies meet at your local school. Is there a PTA or Social Committee? Perhaps there are Drama, Writing or Sports Groups.

Study tips

1 Before going to the school either write down what you want to say, or practise it with someone.

2 How would you describe your child's personality? Describe him or her in writing or **orally**. Are there any words you don't know in English? Use a dictionary.

3 Is there anything about your child you would need to tell his/her teacher? Can you say it in English?

Glossary

allergic	to have a bad reaction (rash, sneezing etc) to something you eat or drink
behaviour	the way you do things, well or badly
contact	to write or telephone
coping	managing something difficult
culture	the art and beliefs of a group of people
customs	the actions of a group of people
flu	short for influenza, an illness with sneezing, aches and fever
history	study of the past
infant school	school for children from 4 years old
measles	illness with rash and fever (German measles is rubella)
medical	a health check by a doctor
mumps	illness with a swollen neck
orally	by speaking or talking
personality	what a person is like, how he/she does things
progress	to make progress, to get better at something
reception	the first class in an infant school

register	to put on a list of names
role	job or part to be played
shy	timid, quiet, afraid of people not known
strengths	things someone is good at
struggling	trying hard to do something that is difficult
subject	something you learn at school or college, such as English, History, or Science
topics	things to talk or write about, themes
vegetarian	not eating meat
worries	feelings that something may be wrong or that something bad will happen

Colloquial phrases

pay attention . . .	Pay attention, please. (Listen to me, please.) Is everyone paying attention?
pleased to . . .	I'm pleased to say that she is doing well. (I'm glad she is doing well.) I'm pleased to hear that. I'm pleased to see you here.
getting on . . .	She's getting on well at school. (She's doing well at school.) I don't know how he's getting on, I never see him. My mother's getting on now. (My mother is getting old now.)
settling in . . .	We are settling in to our new house. I don't feel settled in yet.

7　Finding Work

One-minute summary

In this chapter you will learn how to:

- register at the Job Centre – learn how to claim Jobseeker's Allowance, prepare for an interview with an Employment Service Adviser, know what he or she will ask you, and prepare your answers and ask questions
- phone an employer about a job – phone about jobs advertised, and make **speculative** calls
- improve your job interview skills – learn which questions you might be asked, and prepare suitable answers
- ask questions about areas such as – uniform, clothing and **equipment**, working hours, salary, tax and **National Insurance**, and holidays.

Registering at the Job Centre

Language practice

I'd like to make an appointment for a new **claim**, please.
I would like an interview with an Employment Service Adviser.
My National Insurance number is _____.
I'm looking for work as a _____.
I'm looking for work in a factory/shop/hotel.
I can work normal office hours.
I can/can't work evenings/weekends/**shifts**.
Are there any suitable vacancies at the moment?
I can/can't travel to work.
Who are the main employers in this area?
Are there any training opportunities?
When will I get my first payment?
How is it paid?

When do I **sign on**?
Are there any **schemes** or **programmes** I can join?

Real-life conversation

Scene: at the Job Centre

Claudia:	Hello. I have an appointment with an Employment Service Adviser.
Clerk:	What's your name?
Claudia:	Claudia Hernandez.
Clerk:	Ah, yes. Take a seat here, please. Mr Steele will be with you in a minute.
Mr Steele:	Right. Claudia, is it?
Claudia:	Yes.
Mr Steele:	Do you mind if I call you Claudia?
Claudia:	No, not at all.
Mr Steele:	Okay, Claudia, you want to make a claim.
Claudia:	Yes.
Mr Steele:	Have you filled in a claim form?
Claudia:	Yes. Here it is.

Mr Steele:	Thank you. I'll just check you haven't missed anything. No. That looks fine. So you arrived here last Friday, did you?
Claudia:	Yes.
Mr Steele:	And how long are you planning to stay here?
Claudia:	Permanently.
Mr Steele:	What kind of employment are you looking for?
Claudia:	I'm looking for a full-time job as a hairdresser.
Mr Steele:	I see. Do you have **experience** in this **line** of work?
Claudia:	Yes. I worked as a hairdresser in Spain for five years. I have a National Certificate in hairdressing.
Mr Steele:	So you're **qualified** and have experience. That's good. What hours are you available for work?
Claudia:	I can work anytime.
Mr Steele:	Including evenings and weekends?
Claudia:	Yes. I don't have any **ties**.
Mr Steele:	Good. What plans do you have as to how you will **go about** finding work?
Claudia:	Well, I will look in the local newspapers and have a walk around the town to see if any of the **salons** are looking for staff. Do you know if you have any vacancies in hairdressing at the moment?
Mr Steele:	There was one, but it was filled last week. I think there might be one in Bristol. Could you travel there?
Claudia:	Yes, if I can get a bus.
Mr Steele:	There's a regular bus service. I'll give you the details of the job later.
Claudia:	Thank you. Do you know any hairdressing salons in the area?

Mr Steele:	There are quite a few in the town. **If I were you**, I'd look in the *Yellow Pages*.
Claudia:	*Yellow Pages?*
Mr Steele:	Yes. It's a business telephone directory. It will give you details of all the salons in the area and you can ring them to see if they have any vacancies.
Claudia:	Oh, yes. That is a good idea.
Mr Steele:	Now we are going to **draw up** a **Jobseeker's Agreement**. When are you available to start work?
Claudia:	Straight away.
Mr Steele:	Good. And you've already said you can work at any time and there is nothing which might **restrict** your availability.
Claudia:	That's right.
Mr Steele:	Which area could you work in?
Claudia:	Anywhere I can reach by bus within an hour.
Mr Steele:	Okay. You will have to prove that you are actively seeking work. We ask you to keep a record of everything you do: phone calls, applications, visits to the Job Centre and so on.
Claudia:	Yes. I understand.
Mr Steele:	Are there any other jobs you would consider?
Claudia:	Yes. I would consider working in a shop or restaurant.
Mr Steele:	Now, you will have to come here and **sign on** once a fortnight. Your first signing on will be next Wednesday at 10.30, then every two weeks.
Claudia:	Next Wednesday, is that the fourteenth?
Mr Steele:	Yes, it is.
Claudia:	And when will I get my first payment?
Mr Steele:	You should allow a week to ten days for

the first one then they should arrive two days after you sign on. You can have it paid directly into your bank account or we can send you a Giro.

Claudia: A Giro?

Mr Steele: Yes. It's like a cheque. You take it to the post office and they will give you money for it.

Claudia: I don't have a bank account, so I'd like a Giro, please.

Mr Steele: Which post office would you like to cash it in?

Claudia: The post office here in the town.

Mr Steele: Okay. Do you have any questions?

Claudia: Yes. If I can't get a job I'd like to do further training. Could you advise me on that?

Mr Steele: Yes, of course.

- *Note* – Procedures may change or differ from the above example.

Phoning an employer about a job

Language practice

Can I speak to _____, please?

Can I have **extension** _____, please?

Hello, I'd like to apply for the post of _____.

It was advertised in _____.

I'm interested in _____.

Could you send me an application form?

What are the hours/wages?

What kind of work is it?

I've worked as/in a _____, for _____.

Real-life conversation

Scene: Laurent's home

Laurent:	Hello. Could I speak to Peter Martindale, please?
Receptionist:	Can I ask who's calling?
Laurent:	Yes. My name's Laurent Sorel. I'm interested in the vacancy for head chef.
Receptionist:	I'll put you through.
P. Martindale:	Hello, Peter Martindale. How can I help you?
Laurent:	Hello. My name's Laurent Sorel. I'd like to apply for the post of head chef.
P. Martindale:	Do you have any experience in the catering trade?
Laurent:	Yes. I worked in a large hotel in Paris for five years as a pastry chef.
P. Martindale:	A pastry chef. That's good. Do you have experience in other areas of catering?
Laurent:	Yes. My parents owned a restaurant and I helped them with the cooking.
P. Martindale:	That's good. We are interviewing on Friday morning. Could you come then?
Laurent:	Yes. What time would you like to see me?
P. Martindale:	Eleven thirty. Do you know where we are?

Laurent:	Yes.
P. Martindale:	We'll send you an application form today. Could you complete it and bring it with you?
Laurent:	Yes.
P. Martindale:	Okay then, Laurent. I **look forward to** seeing you on Friday.
Laurent:	Thank you very much. Goodbye.

Improving your job interview skills

Language practice

- *Note* – These are questions you might be asked by the interviewer. Possible answers are suggested, although you should answer as you feel suitable.

Why did you apply for this job?
It sounds interesting.
There are good career **prospects**.
I want to **specialise** in _____.

What do you know about this company/firm?

- *Note* – You need to prepare for this question by looking at any brochures or advertising material. If possible ask someone who works there already.

I know they are a large/small, local/national/international company.

It was founded in _____.
They are well established/well known.

What work have you done before?
I was a _____for/at_____ for_____ years.
I was responsible for _____.
My duties were _____.
(include any **voluntary** work)

What can you tell me about yourself?
I went to school/college in _____.
I studied _____ at _____.
I'm single/married with _____ child/children.
I worked as _____ (see previous question)
I like _____ (hobbies and interests – See chapter 1)
I'm **outgoing, punctual, reliable.**
I'm well **qualified**
I have **considerable** experience of _____.
I can drive/have my own car etc.

What are your strengths and weaknesses?
I'm (very) good at _____.
I'm weak/not so good at _____.

What can you offer us?
(see the answers to the last two questions)

What do you do in your spare time? (see chapter 1)
I like/play _____.
I'm a member of _____.
I'm studying at _____.

Do you have any health problems that might affect your ability to do the job?
No. None that I am aware of.

(If you do say what the problem is, say what medication you might be taking.)

Real-life conversation

Scene: A travel agency

Mr. Wong:	You're Samuel, is that right?
Samuel:	Yes.
Mr Wong:	Pleased to meet you, Samuel. Take a seat.
Samuel:	Thank you.
Mr Wong:	Could you tell me about yourself?
Samuel:	Well, I left school two years ago and worked in a factory for four months before I was made **redundant**. I was **unemployed** for six months, so I decided to go to college to study Leisure and Tourism. My father was in the army, so I had travelled a lot and I thought this might be useful.
Mr Wong:	I'm sure it was. Do you speak many languages?
Samuel:	Yes. I'm **fluent** in German and Spanish. I'm taking Italian at evening classes. I learned French at school, too.
Mr Wong:	Excellent. What do you do in your spare time?
Samuel:	As I said, I'm studying Italian. I play basketball and I'm in a cycling club.
Mr Wong:	Very good. Tell me, Samuel, why did you apply for this job?
Samuel:	Well it sounded interesting and I want a job with career prospects. I would like to get experience as travel agent, then train for management.
Mr Wong:	I see. Well we do have an excellent management training programme, but you haven't any experience of working in a travel agency.

Samuel:	As part of my college programme I did a work placement at Holidays You Go. I really enjoyed it. I did some admin, answered the phones and helped with bookings.
Mr Wong:	Would they give you a reference?
Samuel:	Yes. They said they would. I can get one from my college tutor too.
Mr Wong:	Good. What do you think you could offer our firm, Samuel?
Samuel:	Well, obviously my knowledge of languages and the amount of travelling would be useful. I enjoy working with the public and I'm reliable. I'm fit and healthy.
Mr Wong:	What do you think might be your weaknesses?
Samuel:	I'm a little nervous on the telephone. I think I need more training in telephone enquiries.
Mr Wong:	Our training will cover that. People usually become more confident with practice.

Asking questions at an interview

Language practice

Do you provide a uniform/clothing?
What is the holiday entitlement?   or
How many days holiday do you get?
Do you provide training?   or
What training do you provide?
How much **overtime** am I likely to get?
Is there a **union**?
Is there a pension **scheme**?
Would I get paid weekly or monthly?

How are wages paid? (for example by cheque, cash or
directly into the bank)
Is tax/National Insurance **deducted**?
What are the opportunities for promotion?
Do you have any sports and social facilities?
Do you have a **crèche**?
Do you offer childcare?

Real-life conversation

Scene: The Grand Hotel

Mr Sadiq:	Are there any questions you would like to ask about the job?
Helen:	Yes. Do you provide a uniform?
Mr Sadiq:	Yes. The reception staff is all provided with uniforms. You will get a jacket, two skirts and three or four blouses.
Helen:	What about training?
Mr Sadiq:	We will provide a three-day **initial** training course. After that we will provide additional training if necessary.
Helen:	Do you have a pension scheme?
Mr Sadiq:	Yes. We offer a company pension scheme to all employees.
Helen:	That's good. Would I be paid weekly or monthly?
Mr Sadiq:	You'd be paid monthly directly into the bank.
Helen:	And is tax and National Insurance deducted?
Mr Sadiq:	Yes. They will both be deducted at source.
Helen:	That's good. Do you have any sports and social activities?
Mr Sadiq:	The hotel has facilities, but I'm afraid they are for the use of guests only. There are a few sports clubs in the town, oh

and a swimming pool. You said you liked swimming, didn't you?

Helen: Yes.

Mr Sadiq: Have you any other questions?

Helen: You mentioned overtime earlier. How much overtime am I likely to be asked to do?

Mr Sadiq: Well, obviously if we were short staffed because of holidays or illness we would ask you to come in. We might also ask you to do extra hours during the busy periods, the summer, Christmas and Easter.

Helen: Yes. That reminds me, what is the holiday entitlement?

Mr Sadiq: You are entitled to six weeks a year. If you work bank holidays you get double time.

Helen: Thank you. I don't think there was anything else I needed to ask.

Language transfer

If I were you (used to offer advice to someone, to give your opinion on what you think he/she should do)

If I were you I'd use the *Yellow Pages*.
If I were you I'd get my hair cut.
If I were you I wouldn't go shopping today. The shops will be really busy.

To look forward to (to wait for something with pleasure, to anticipate something pleasing)

I look forward to seeing you.
We are looking forward to our holiday this year.

It can also be used in the negative to show that you are dreading something:

I'm not looking forward to meeting him. I've heard he is a horrible man.

Helping you learn

Progress questions

1 Where can you find job advertisements? Make a list of as many places as possible.

2 Prepare some possible answers to questions you might be asked at an interview. Practise them.

3 Make a list of any questions you might like to ask. Are there any I haven't given in the chapter?

Discussion points

1 Equal Opportunities means that no employer should **discriminate** against a person because of his/her age, sex, religion or culture? Do you think employers do discriminate?

2 Do you think the way you appear at an interview (your clothes, hair) are important?

3 How difficult do you think it is to find a job?

Practical assignments

1 Try a mock interview with someone you know well.

2 Visit your local Job Centre and ask for advice on finding a job. You might also ask for some leaflets. Useful ones may include:

Jobseekers Allowance: Helping you back to work
People Going Abroad or Coming from Abroad
Just the Job: A guide to what your Job Centre can do for you.

You may also be able to get leaflets in your first language.

Study tips

1 Keep a record of every job you apply for: include the job advert, a copy of the completed application form and any letters or information about the job or company.

2 Prepare yourself well for your interview. Plan what you have to say. Read your application form or curriculum vitae before you go. Is there anything there they are likely to ask you about?

3 Your local Job Centre can provide special help for people whose first language is not English in the form of pre-vocational training. They might also help you to fill in the forms and give you information in your first language.

Glossary

availability	time when you are free to do something
claim	application, a request for something
crèche	nursery, place where children are cared for
curriculum vitae	a list of personal details sent to an employer, telling him/her about your work, education, interests and skills.
deducted	taken off, subtracted
discriminate	to dislike or favour a person or group of people because of their religion, sex or beliefs
draw up	to make or write
equipment	things you use to do something
experience	to have experience means to have done something before
initial	the first
Jobseekers' Agreement	document saying that you are looking for work and are available to work
line	type, area
National Insurance	money paid to the government from your wages so that you will get a pension

pension scheme	paying money from your wages so that you will get a payment when you are old
pre-vocational	before work
programme	see scheme, the same meaning
qualified	having a certificate, diploma or degree
restrict	make smaller, limit
salon	place where a hairdresser works
scheme	a course organised for a special group of people
shifts	see glossary, chapter 1
sign on	claim Jobseekers' Agreement or state benefit
specialise	to become an expert in something, to study or work in one subject
speculative	speculative calls are calls made to an employer to ask if they have any vacancies
ties	things or people that might stop you from doing something
union	a group of people who protect the rights of workers

Colloquial phrases

go about. . .	How do I go about finding a flat? (How do I start looking for a flat?)
	How do you go about job applications?
	How could I go about meeting her?
if I were you. . .	If I were you, I'd do it later.
	If I were you, I'd wait.
	I wouldn't do it, not if I were you.
to look forward to. . .	I'm looking forward to my birthday.
	I'm not looking forward to next week.

8 At the Bank and Post Office

One-minute summary

In this chapter you will learn how to:

■ send parcels and letters within the UK and abroad, ask for **airmail** and **surface** post, and ask to send a letter by **registered** mail

■ pay bills – ask for **official** forms and to pay bills, ask for application forms for Visas and passports, and tax your car or vehicle

■ open a bank or post office account, open a **deposit** account, open a **current** account and ask to apply for an **overdraft** or **mortgage**

■ make deposits, **withdrawals** and **transfers** – pay cash or cheques into your account, withdraw money from your account, and transfer money from one account to another.

Sending parcels and letters

Language practice

Can I have _____ first class stamp(s), please?

Can I have _____ second class stamps(s), please?

● *Note* – First class post is more expensive, but letters are delivered more quickly.

I'd like to send this parcel to _____.

How much is it by airmail?

How much is it by surface mail?

I'd like to send it by registered mail/**express** delivery.

Real-life conversation

Scene: In the Post Office

Assistant: Can I help you?

Amrit: Hello. I'd like to send this parcel to Pakistan.

Assistant: Can you put it on the scales, please.

Amrit: Of course.

Assistant: Do you want to send it airmail?

Amrit: How much will it be?

Assistant: Two pounds twelve.

Amrit: Yes. That's okay.

Assistant: What's in it?

Amrit: It's a present.

Assistant: Can you tell me what's in it? I need to fill in a **Customs Declaration Form**.

Amrit: Oh, I see. There's a calendar, some handkerchiefs and shirt.

Assistant: What's the **value**?

Amrit: Er, let me see. About fifteen pounds.

Assistant: Can you sign that please.

Amrit: Yes. I'd like to send this letter by registered mail, please.

Assistant: Certainly.

Amrit: And could I have three first class and five second class stamps?

Asking for official forms

Language practice

Could I have an application form for: a British Visitor's
Passport?
a visa?
a UK driving licence?

I'd like to tax my car/van/motorbike etc.
Here is my registration document and insurance certificate.
I want to pay this gas/electric/telephone bill.

Real-life conversation

Scene: At the Post Office

Carmen:	Hello. I'd like to tax my car, please.
Assistant:	Have you filled in the form?
Carmen:	Yes. There you are. And here's my **registration document** and insurance certificate.
Assistant:	Do you want to take it for six months or a year?
Carmen:	A year, please. It works out cheaper that way, doesn't it?
Assistant:	Yes.
Carmen:	Can I pay by cheque?
Assistant:	Yes. Can you make it payable to Post Office Counters?
Carmen:	I'd like to pay my electricity and telephone bills too.
Assistant:	How do you want to pay them?
Carmen:	I've got fifty pounds of electricity stamps and thirty pounds of telephone stamps. I'll pay the **balance** in cash.
Assistant:	Anything else?
Carmen:	No. That's all, thank you.

Opening a bank account

Language practice

I'd like to open a current account/**joint** account/deposit account.

I'd like to apply for a mortgage/overdraft/loan.

Real-life conversation

Scene: At the bank

Mario:	I'd like to open an account, please.
Cashier:	**Is that a** current or deposit account?
Mario:	A savings account.
Cashier:	Do you require a cheque book or cashpoint card?
Mario:	No. We just want to save for a holiday.
Cashier:	A joint deposit account?
Mario:	Yes.
Cashier:	Do you have some money to open the account?
Mario:	Yes. I have fifty pounds cash.
Cashier:	Good. This is your passbook. The **interest rate** will automatically adjust depending on how much you have in the account.
Mario:	Oh. That's good. There's something else. I'd like to apply for a mortgage, please.

Cashier: Certainly. I'll make you an appointment
              with our mortgage adviser.

Making deposits, withdrawals and transfers

Language practice

I'd like to withdraw _____, please.
I'd like to pay this into my account, please.
I'd like to transfer money from my _____ account to
my _____ account, please.
In fives/tens/twenties, please.

Real-life conversation

Scene: At the bank

Rosa: I'd like to pay these cheques into my
              current account, please.
Cashier: Have you filled in a deposit slip?
Rosa: No. I didn't know I had to.
Cashier: If you could just fill that in, please.
Rosa: There you are. And I'd like to transfer a
              hundred pounds from my cheque account
              to my deposit account.
Cashier: Certainly. Could you sign this, please?
Rosa: And I'd like to withdraw fifty pounds,
              please.
Cashier: From which account?
Rosa: The current one.
Cashier: Do you have your card?
Rosa: Yes. There you are.
Cashier: Thank you. **How would you like** the cash?
Rosa: Two twenties and a ten, please.
Cashier: Certainly, madam. Thank you very much.

Language transfer

Is that a... (to offer a choice of options)

Is that a current or a deposit account?
Is that a diet or a **regular** coke?
Is that a small, medium or large pizza?

How would you like... (used to offer a choice of options)

How would you like the cash?
How would you like your eggs? Fried or **boiled**?
How would you like your steak? **Rare**, medium or well done?

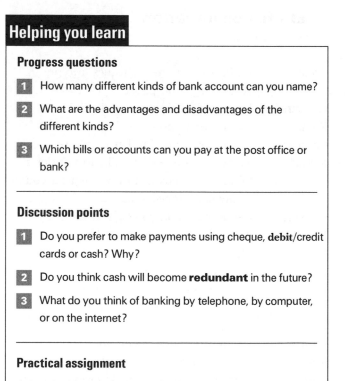

Helping you learn

Progress questions

1. How many different kinds of bank account can you name?

2. What are the advantages and disadvantages of the different kinds?

3. Which bills or accounts can you pay at the post office or bank?

Discussion points

1. Do you prefer to make payments using cheque, **debit**/credit cards or cash? Why?

2. Do you think cash will become **redundant** in the future?

3. What do you think of banking by telephone, by computer, or on the internet?

Practical assignment

Ask at the bank or post office for a few withdrawal and deposit slips and practise filling them in.

Study tips

1 Practise filling in official forms beforehand if you need to. Photocopies are useful.

2 The post office has many useful free leaflets. Take any you think would be useful to read.

Glossary

airmail	letters or parcels sent by aeroplane
balance	an amount still to be paid
current	an account with a chequebook
customs declaration form	a small form, used when a parcel is going abroad, showing what is in it
debit card	see glossary, chapter 4
deposit	to put money into a bank account (see chapter 3 for a different meaning)
deposit account	a savings account
diet	with low sugar or fat
express	very fast
insurance	service where money is paid if something is lost, stolen or damaged
insurance certificate	a paper showing that a vehicle has been insured
interest rate	sum of money given to you by the bank when you save, or taken by the bank when you lend
joint	in the names of two or more people
mortgage	money borrowed to buy a house
official forms	government forms, such as a passport, car tax, driving licence
overdraft	a small loan from the bank when you take out more money than you put in
rare	cooked a little, red in the middle
redundant	not needed (see glossary, chapter 8)
registered mail	a service used for mail which is urgent (needed quickly) or valuable (worth a lot of money)

registration document	an official document showing who owns a car or vehicle
regular	normal, ordinary
surface mail	letters and parcels sent by boat, train etc.
withdrawal	money taken out of a bank account

Colloquial phrases

How would you like . . .	How would you like the parcel wrapped? (How do you wish the parcel to be wrapped?)
	How would you like to come on holiday with me?
	How would you like a trip to London?
Is that a . . .	Is that a promise? (Will you promise me?)
	So you agree to come – is that a promise?
Are you sure?	Are you sure you want to come? (Do you really want to come?)
	Are you sure you sent the cheque?
	Are you sure you have enough money?

Using the Telephone

In this chapter you will learn how to:

■ ask for the person you need – introduce yourself, and know what to say if he/she is not available

■ leave a message on an answering machine – leave a message with confidence, make sure you give the right information so that you will be called back, and practise some useful messages

■ order goods by phone – order take-away foods, and order mail order goods

■ deal with wrong numbers or **nuisance** calls.

Asking for the person you need

Language practice

Hello, this is _____. Can I speak to _____, please?
Could you tell me when he/she would be in/back/available?
I'll call back later.
Could you ask him/her to call me?
My number is _____.
I'll be there until _____.
Could I leave a message?

Real-life conversation

Scene: Mr Asakura's office

Hidetoshi: Hello. This is Hidetoshi Asakura. Can I speak to Mr Suzuki, please?

Receptionist: I'm sorry, Mr Suzuki is in a meeting at the moment.

Hidetoshi:	It's quite important. Could I leave a message?
Receptionist:	Certainly.
Hidetoshi:	Could you ask him to call Hidetoshi Asakura at Head Office. My extension number is 7732.
Receptionist:	Certainly, Mr Asakura. I'll give him your message.
Hidetoshi:	Thank you very much.
Receptionist:	You're welcome. Goodbye.
Hidetoshi:	Goodbye.

Leaving a message on an answering machine

Language practice

Hello. This is _____ speaking.

This is a message for _____.

Could you ring me, please?

I'll be in all morning/afternoon/day/evening.

Could you ring before _____ if possible?

Real-life conversation

Scene: Rashpal's home

Answerphone: Hello. This is the home of Peter and
Susan Foster. I'm afraid we are not able
to take your call at the moment, but if
you'd like to leave your name and
number after the tone, we'll ring you
back...beep.

Rashpal: Hello. This is Rashpal. I have a message
for Susan. I need to speak to you about
the school visit. Could you ring me,
please. My number is _____. I'll
be in all morning, but I'll be out
between two and four this afternoon.
Bye.

Ordering goods by phone

Language practice

Hello. Id like to order a _____, please.
Can I have a _____, please?
Can you deliver it?
My address is _____.
How long will it take?
My reference number is _____.

Real-life conversation (1)

Scene: Frances' house

Take-away: Hello. The Balti House. Can I help you?
Frances: Hello. I'd like to order a meal, please.
Take-away: What would you like?
Frances: A lamb **tikka** and a king prawn
vindaloo, a garlic **nan**, **papadoms** and
two **samosas**.
Take-away: Vegetable or meat samosas?

Frances:	Vegetable, please.
Take-away:	Which rice would you like, **pilau** or boiled?
Frances:	Pilau, please.
Take-away:	Anything else?
Frances:	No. That's all.
Take-away:	Is it a delivery?
Frances:	Yes, please.
Take-away:	What's the address?
Frances:	59 Front Street.
Take-away:	Is that Millbrook?
Frances:	Yes. How long will it be?
Take-away:	About twenty minutes.
Frances:	That's fine. See you then.

Real-life conversation (2)

Scene: Mrs Kaur's house

Woman:	Hello. Clothing Company. Do you wish to place an order?
Mrs Kaur:	Yes.
Woman:	Can I have your customer reference number?
Mrs Kaur:	Yes. It's 86598453.

Woman:	Is that Mrs Kaur?
Mrs Kaur:	Yes.
Woman:	Beechtree House, Millbrook?
Mrs Kaur:	Yes.
Woman:	What's the number of your first item?
Mrs Kaur:	LJH35986218
Woman:	What size?
Mrs Kaur:	14.
Woman:	Next item?
Mrs Kaur:	LJH3637795
Woman:	What size?
Mrs Kaur:	14
Woman:	Next?
Mrs Kaur:	That's all, thank you.
Woman:	The blouse will be two to three weeks. The skirt will be here by Wednesday.
Mrs Kaur:	Thank you.

Dealing with wrong numbers and nuisance calls

Language practice

I'm sorry, there's no one here by that name.
I think you have a wrong number.
I'm sorry, I'm not interested. I'm busy at the moment.
I'd rather you didn't call again.
Please don't call again.

Real-life situation

Scene: Ruth's house

Ruth:	Hello.
Caller:	Hello. Can I speak to Nick, please.
Ruth:	There's no one here by that name. I think you have a wrong number.
Caller:	Well this is the number he gave me. Is that 7798659?

Ruth:	Yes, but there's no one here called Nick.
Caller:	Are you sure?
Ruth:	Yes. Goodbye.

(one minute later...)

Ruth:	Hello.
Caller:	Hello. Can I speak to Nick.
Ruth:	I've already told you, there's no-one called Nick here. You must have the wrong number.
Caller:	Oh not you again. Where's Nick? Nick told me to phone.
Ruth:	I've told you, there's no Nick here. I'm busy at the moment. Please don't call again. Goodbye.

Language transfer

I'd rather you didn't...(used to ask someone to stop doing something)

I'd rather you didn't call again.
Do you mind if I smoke? **I'd rather you didn't.**
I'd rather you didn't park your car there. It's in front of my garage.

Helping you learn

Progress questions

1 You want to speak to someone on the telephone, but when you call he/she is in a meeting? There are several things you might say. What are they?

2 What information should you leave on an answering machine to be sure you will be called back?

3 What could you say to a nuisance caller?

Discussion points

1 Have you ever received a **malicious** call? What did you do?

2 What are the **advantages** and **disadvantages** of ordering goods by mail order?

Practical assignments

1 Place an order by telephone. It could be for food, clothing, books or anything you like.

2 If you know someone who has an answering machine, arrange to phone him or her and leave a message.

Study tips

1 If you phone somebody and get an answering machine, don't **panic**! Put the receiver down and prepare what you want to say. Write it down if it helps. Then phone again. You will feel much more confident.

2 Read the information at the beginning of the telephone directory. There are many services you can use, such as **Operator Service** and **Directory Enquiries**. There is also lots of helpful advice.

3 Telephone companies often send customers leaflets about their services. Read them. If there is a service which you feel would benefit you, call and ask about it. You might save money!

Glossary

advantages	good points
directory enquiries	a service to help you find a telephone number or code
disadvantages	bad points
malicious	nasty, unkind, threatening
nan	Indian bread

nuisance	unwanted, annoying
operator service	a service that will help you if you are having problems making a call
panic	to be frightened, worried, not sure what to do
papadoms	fried wheat cake eaten with curry
pilau	fried rice, usually with vegetables, spices etc
samosa	Indian pastry filled with spiced meat and/or vegetables
tikka	a mild curry
vindaloo	a hot curry

Colloquial phrases

I'd rather...	I'd rather go dancing. (I would prefer to go dancing.)
	I'd rather go home.
	Wouldn't you rather come with me?
	I'd rather not.

Emergencies

In this chapter you will learn how to:

- make a 999 call – ask for the emergency service you want, say where the emergency is, say what the emergency is, say where you are and give the telephone number
- describe an emergency – describe a number of emergency situations, say what happened and when, and give details of any **injuries** or **dangers**
- ask a stranger for help – **approach** a stranger and get his/her attention, explain the situation quickly, and tell him/her how he/she can help
- deal with going to hospital in an emergency – know what questions you may be asked, and answer them quickly.

Making a 999 call
Language practice

- *Note* – in an emergency dial 999. Calls are free. You can also dial 112.

Fire/police/ambulance/**coastguard**/**mountain rescue**, please.
My house is on fire. There are people **trapped** inside.
There has been an accident.
Somebody is **drowning**.
Somebody is badly injured.
Someone is **unconscious**.
Someone has fallen from a ladder/from a tree/from a roof.
I think he/she has broken his/her arm/leg/neck.
He/she has lost a lot of blood.
My husband is having/has had a **fit**/heart attack etc
My wife has swallowed some **poison**/medicine/tablets
I'm at _____. The telephone number is _____.

Real-life conversation

Scene: Monica's neighbour's house

Operator:	Emergency. Which service do you require?
Monica:	Fire, please.
Operator:	I'll put you through.
Fire Service:	Hello. Fire Service.
Monica:	Hello. My house is on fire. My little boy...
Fire Service:	He's in the house?
Monica:	Yes.
Fire Service:	Okay. What's your address, caller?
Monica:	The Schoolhouse, Millbrook.
Fire Service:	Where are you phoning from?
Monica:	My neighbours. The number is _____.
Fire Service:	The Brigade will be here soon. Don't go back into the house.
Monica:	I won't. Thank you.

Describing an emergency

Language practice

See 'Making a 999 call' for examples of emergencies.

It happened twenty minutes ago.
It happened half an hour ago.
I **have just** found him/her.
He/she has a heart problem/**epilepsy**.
He/she is in the garden/kitchen/bathroom.
Follow me.

Real-life conversation

Scene: outside William's house

Ambulance man:	William Davis?
William:	Yes.
Ambulance man:	Your wife has fallen from a ladder?
William:	Yes. She was painting the ceiling and lost **balance**.
Ambulance man:	Where is she?
William:	In the living room. Follow me.
Ambulance man:	When did it happen?
William:	I don't know. I was in the garden. I found her just before I called you.
Ambulance man:	Was she unconscious when you found her?
William:	Yes.
Ambulance man:	**We'd better** get her to hospital. She's lost a lot of blood from that wound.
William:	Yes.

Asking a stranger for help

Language practice

See 'Making a 999 call' for examples of emergencies.

Excuse me. There's been an accident. I need your help.

Can you phone a doctor?
Can you stay here until I get back?
Can I use your telephone?
Do you know where I can find a telephone?

Real-life conversation

Scene: At the front door of Mr Chazan's house

Mr Chazan:	Hello.
Mr Evans:	Excuse me. There's been an accident. Can you help me, please?
Mr Chazan:	Well, I'm on my way to work.
Mr Evans:	Please help. My son is badly hurt. I think he's broken his neck.
Mr Chazan:	Oh, I see, but what can I do?
Mr Evans:	Do you have a telephone?
Mr Chazan:	Oh yes, yes. Of course. Come in. There it is.
Mr Evans:	Thank you.

Going to hospital in an emergency

Language practice

See 'Making a 999 call' for examples of emergencies.

The following questions may be asked at the hospital. They are not questions that you will ask.

What has happened?
When did it happen?
What is the name and address of the patient?
What is his/her date of birth?
Who is his/her **GP**?
What is his/her religion?
What **medication** is the patient taking?
Is he/she **allergic** to any medication?
What is your name?

Who is the patient's **next of kin**?
Who should be **contacted** to give **consent** for any **treatment**?

Real-life conversation

Scene: Accident and Emergency, Millbrook General

Nurse:	Hello. I'm staff nurse Clark. What has happened?
Bruno:	My son has a **fever** and is very **drowsy**. He also has a **rash** and has been **vomiting**.
Nurse:	How long has he been ill?
Bruno:	I took him to see the doctor this morning because he had a fever, but the rash and vomiting just started this evening. I called the doctor and he said to bring him here.
Nurse:	Has he been taking any medication?
Bruno:	Yes. He has been taking **paracetamol** and **penicillin**.
Nurse:	Is he allergic to any medicines?
Bruno:	Not as far as I know.
Nurse:	What is your son's name?
Bruno:	Paul Martin.
Nurse:	And his date of birth?
Bruno:	Twenty-seventh of September, he's 7 years old.
Nurse:	Who's his GP?
Bruno:	GP?
Nurse:	His doctor?
Bruno:	Oh. Doctor Chatterjee.
Nurse:	Millbrook Health Centre?
Bruno:	Yes.
Nurse:	I'm going to get a doctor to come and see Paul.
Bruno:	Thank you.

- *Note* – A fever, vomiting and a change in **mood** are all symptoms of a serious **disease** called **meningitis**. Other symptoms are a red rash, which does not fade when you press a glass against it, **dislike** of lights, a bad headache and painful neck. If you think anyone may have meningitis, call a doctor.

Language transfer

to have just... (used to say something happened a short time ago)

I **have just** found her.
I **have just** been told that I have got a new job.
We **have just** heard the bad news.

to have better... (used to say that something must be done)
We **had better** get her to hospital.

He **had better** hurry up. He is going to miss the train.
You **had better** put your coat on. It is really cold.

Helping you learn

Progress questions

1 What information do you need to give when you make an emergency phone call?

2 What would you be asked at a hospital in an emergency?

Discussion points

1 Have you ever been in an emergency situation? What happened?

2 When would you call an ambulance rather than a doctor?

Practical assignments

1 Practise making emergency phone calls with a friend, teacher or relative. *Never* dial an emergency number unless it is an emergency.

2 If you have children, discuss with them what they should do in an emergency. Get them to practise, too.

3 Find out as much as you can about what to do in emergency situations. Your local library will have books and leaflets.

Study tips

1 Read as much as you can about how to handle emergency situations. The advice might save your life or the life of someone else.

2 Watch television programmes which show emergency situations. You will learn a lot from them too.

Glossary

approach	go up to, talk to
balance	having an even weight
coastguard	someone who helps people in danger at sea
consent	saying that something can happen
contacted	telephoned
dangers	things, which could hurt you
dislike	not liking
drowsy	tired, wanting to sleep
drowning	in danger in water
epilepsy	illness causing fits, shaking
fade	to go lighter or paler
fever	high body temperature.
fit (to have a)	to suffer shakes and become unconscious
GP	general practitioner, family doctor
injured	having been hurt, having cuts, wounds, broken bones etc.
injuries	cuts, wounds, broken bones etc.
meningitis	a serious disease, an infection of the brain
mood	the way a person feels or acts
mountain rescue	a service to help people hurt in the mountains

operator	the person who takes phone calls and helps you get the person or service you need
paracetamol	a drug that takes away pain and lowers fever
penicillin	a drug that fights infection
rash	lots of small, red spots on the skin
trapped	unable to get out of somewhere
treatment	something that is done to a person to help them
unconscious	not aware of anything, unable to see hear, talk etc
vomiting	sickness, bringing up food and drink from the mouth

Colloquial phrases

to have better. . .	We had better go now. (We should go now.)
	I'd better phone the hospital first.
	You'd better not, we'll be late.
to have just. . .	I have just got back. (I returned very recently.)
	I have just arrived.
	He has just died.
	She has just posted a letter.
	They have just managed to find him.
	His neighbours have just arrived.

11 **Understanding Regional Speech**

One-minute summary

In this chapter you will learn about **regional** accent and speech and about languages other than English which are native to Britain. You will learn how to talk about:

■ regional accents – understand how accents affect English **pronunciation**, and how greetings vary from region to region; you will lean some commonly used words and **phrases**, and how to ask for clarification if you don't understand

■ other British native languages – where **native** languages such as **Welsh** and **Gaelic** are used, why and in which situations native languages may be used, how Welsh, Scottish and Irish words have become **incorporated** into English. how to overcome the fact that there may be no direct English equivalent.

Regional accents

Language practice

I don't recognise your accent.
What part of Britain are you from?
I'm not familiar with that word/phrase/expression.
I'm sorry, could you repeat that?
I didn't catch what you said.
I'm afraid I still don't understand. Could you explain to me?
I'm really interested in what you're telling me, but I'm having difficulty with your accent.
Could you speak a little more slowly?
I've never heard that word/phrase/expression before. What does it mean?

- *Note:* Never ask someone to speak more clearly, this could cause **offence**.

Real-life conversation

Scene: At a party. Fernanda sees her brother José, who is with Dave, James and Rashpal

Fernanda: Hi, José, are these the friends from college you were telling me about?

José: Yes. This is Fernanda, my sister. Fernanda, this is Dave, James and Rashpal.

Fernanda: Rashpal's an Indian name, isn't it?

Rashpal: Yes, my parents are Indian, but I'm a **Scouser**, born and bred in Liverpool. James here is a **Brummie** and Dave's a **Cockney**, aren't you, mate?

Fernanda: James, you're from Birmingham, a Brummie he said?

James: That's sound.

Fernanda: Sound, I'm not familiar with that word.

James: That's right. Soz. I mean sorry.

Fernanda: So, sound means good and soz means sorry in Birmingham.

Rashpal: I dunno (don't know) a blind word he says. Yer wanna (you want to) give yer (your) chin a rest, James.

Fernanda: I've never heard that expression before. What does it mean?

Rashpal: I'm telling him to purra (put a) zip in it.

Fernanda: I'm afraid I still don't understand. Could you explain to me?

Rashpal: Give yer chin a rest, means not to talk so much, zip up your mouth. (He moves two fingers from one side of his mouth to the other as if zipping it up.)

Fernanda: (laughing) Oh, I see.

Dave:	Take a **butcher's** over there, here's Geordie. 'Allo, **china**.
Fernanda:	Take a Butchers?
José:	Butcher's Hook, look. It's Cockney **rhyming slang**. He called Geordie, china. That's rhyming slang too. China plate, mate or friend.
Fernanda:	All these accents and dialects are confusing, aren't they?
José:	You'll soon get used to them.
Geordie:	Hey lads, I didn't na (know) you were gannin oot (going out) the night (tonight), like.
Fernanda:	Can you speak more slowly, I'm having trouble with your accent
Geordie:	I didn't na the lads were gannin oot the night.
Fernanda:	You didn't know they were going out tonight. You weren't expecting to see them.
Geordie:	Correct. And who's this **bonny** lass, then?
José:	It's my sister, Fernanda. Fernanda, this is Mike.
Fernanda:	Now I'm really confused. I thought he was called Geordie.
Geordie:	They call me that cos I **hail** from Newcastle.
Fernanda:	I'm sorry, could you repeat that. I didn't catch what you said.
Geordie:	My name is Mike, but everyone calls me Geordie. I'm from Newcastle, up North.
José:	Geordie is used to describe people from Newcastle.
Fernanda:	I see. Geordie, Scouse, Cockney, Brummie. They're regional dialects.
Dave:	You got any bread, china?
Geordie:	Bread. Oh, bread and honey, money. I divvent knaa aboot this Cockney Slang.

Fernanda:	I'm really interested in what you're telling me, but I'm having difficulty with your accent.
Geordie:	I was explaining what Dave said. He asked if I had any bread. He meant money. Bread is rhyming slang – bread and honey, meaning money.
Dave:	That's right, china. Used all my bread on the old jam jar. (To Fernanda) Jam jar, Danny Marr, car.
James:	How's it going kid?
Geordie:	Aaal reet. Not bad at all.
James:	O'rite. That's sound.
Fernanda:	(laughing) Sound. Nice talking to you all.

Native languages

Language practice

You've got a strong accent.

What part of England/Scotland/Wales/Ireland/Britain are you from?

Do they speak Gaelic/Welsh here/there?

Is _____. spoken here/there?

So you're **bilingual**?

Do you write _____ as well as speak it?

I am Gaelic/Welsh speaking.

Real-life conversation

Scene: Half-time at an international rugby match in Cardiff. Wales are playing Scotland.

Callum:	Hey Kwesi, what are you doing here?
Kwesi:	I came to the match with Aled.
Callum:	Of course, you told me you have a friend, Aled, who is Welsh.
Kwesi:	Aled, come here, you must meet Callum.

Aled:	Hi, Callum. **I take it** you're Scottish? Are you just in Cardiff for the match?
Callum:	No, I'm working here at the moment. I'm here for a few months.
Aled:	You've got a strong accent. What part of Scotland are you from?
Callum:	Oban, up in the Highlands.
Aled:	Do they speak Gaelic up there?
Callum:	Some of them do. I can speak a **wee** bit of the Gaelic. My grandparents speak it all the time.
Aled:	Do they speak English too?
Callum:	Yes, but they prefer to use the Gaelic. That's their first language.
Kwesi:	Aled speaks Welsh.
Callum:	So you're bilingual, like Kwesi?
Aled:	I am indeed. I come from Dyfed. My parents are both Welsh-speaking. We prefer to call our language Cymraeg, though, not Welsh.
Callum:	I noticed lots of young people speak it. It's mainly the older generation who speak Gaelic in Scotland.
Aled:	We do all we can to **preserve** our language, it's part of our culture.
Callum:	Gaelic is mainly used in the north and west, the Highlands and Islands of Scotland. Is Cymraeg used all over Wales?
Aled:	Cymraeg is being used more and more in the south east, but it is the main language used in the west and north of Cymru.
Callum:	Cymru? (Kumree) Is that how you pronounce it?
Aled:	That's right, Cymru. You call Scotland Alba, don't you?
Callum:	Aye, we do. Do you write in both languages?

Aled:	Of course. I studied Cymraeg in school.
Kwesi:	I can't understand him when he speaks to his Welsh friends.
Aled:	I'm sorry. We use English when we can, but sometimes it's easier to express ourselves in our native language.
Kwesi:	I know. I understand that. I often know a word in my language, but can't say it in English.
Callum:	There's Gaelic words like that, sometimes there isn't an equivalent in English.
Aled:	I know what you mean.
Kwesi:	We'd better go, the second half of the match has started.
Callum:	See yous later.
Kwesi/Aled:	See you.
Kwesi:	Did he say yous?
Aled:	Yes, Scottish people often add an s to the plural.
Kwesi:	I see. Come on, I think someone's just scored. Hope it's Wales.

Language transfer

Having difficulty with...unable to understand or make sense of

I'm **having difficulty with** your accent.
I'm **having difficulty with** literacy. (reading, writing)

I take it I understand, I see, I assume

I **take it** you're Scottish.

* *Note*: Sometimes used ironically or to express mild sarcasm.

I take it you're coming with us. (used when someone appears to have invited themselves)

Helping you learn

Progress questions

1 What are the **nicknames** used for people from London, Newcastle, Birmingham and Liverpool? Do you know nicknames for people from other cities? What about Manchester, Glasgow, Aberdeen, etc?

2 What do you know about languages spoken and written in Britain? Is more than one language spoken or written in your home country?

Discussion points

1 What are the differences between language, dialect and accent?

2 Some people believe everyone should speak Queen's English, without local accents. Do you agree? Do you think news reporters and TV/radio presenters should speak without local accents, for example?

3 Sometimes people are judged or discriminated against because of their dialect or accent. Have you experienced this?

Practical assignments

1 Make a list of words and phrases used in the area of Britain in which you live with their meanings and/or their equivalents in English or your native language. You can ask local people to help or use the Internet. Most areas also have books about their local dialect in the library or shops.

2 Find out as much as you can about the **policies** to retain native languages in Britain and/or your home country.

Study tips

1 Use the Internet or reference books to find out more about dialects or languages spoken in different parts of Britain. It might be useful to refer to a map or maps of the areas. You might like to study the history of the dialect/language or compile a list of common words and expressions.

2 Television provides a wonderful opportunity to listen to a range of accents, dialogues and languages. Try to find and listen to programmes where local language or dialect is used.

3 Try to find out as much as possible about the past and present influences on English. Past influences might be historical, for example invaders and immigrants. Present influences might be the media, television, technology etc. Are there words used in English which come originally from your native language? Perhaps there are also English words which have been incorporated into yours.

4 Most areas have books about their local dialect, which you may find useful and fun. You may also like to study the local history of the area in which you live. You can do this by buying or borrowing books, surfing the Net, visiting local museums and places of interest or even joining a Local History Class or group.

Glossary

accent	the way people from a place or region pronounce sounds and words
bilingual	able to write or speak two languages fluently
bonny	a word used in Scotland and Northern England meaning pretty or attractive
Brummie	a person who comes from Birmingham, also the accent and local dialect
butcher's	Cockney rhyming slang, butcher's hook, shortened to butcher's meaning look.
china	fine material from which cups, saucers, plates etc are made
Cockney	a person from London, the accent and dialect spoken there

dialect	type of language spoken in a particular area
discriminated	to be discriminated against is to have someone act or speak negatively about you because of your colour, sex, religion etc
equivalent	same amount
Gaelic	languages native to Scotland, Ireland and the Isle of Man
hail	to come from or live in
incorporate	make part of
influences	things which affect or change something
judge	say whether something is good or bad
nickname	a name given to a person by family or friends, not their real name
offence	to cause offence means to anger and annoy
regional	from a certain area, county or district
rhyming	words with the same end sound, eg, mat, cat and rat.
Scouser	person who comes from Liverpool, also the accent and local dialect
slang	informal or local language
phrases	groups of words, parts of sentences
pronunciation	the way in which a word or sound is said
preserve	keep safe/alive
policies	actions of people and/or their council or government
Queen's English	very formal, correct English.
wee	Scottish for small, or little
Welsh	the language used in Wales, also known as Cymraeg (see note below)

Note: The Welsh people prefer to call themselves Cymry and their country, Cymru. The Scots call their country Alba. The Irish Gaelic name for Ireland, Eire, is often used for the Republic of Ireland.

Metaphor in Spoken English

In this chapter you will learn: some commonly used English **metaphors** and **expressions** used in everyday conversations to describe:

- people's personalities – how people appear to others, how people behave, and how people feel
- work relationships – metaphors connected with money, and metaphors used to describe **colleagues** or **customers**
- personal relationships – how to indicate a relationship is going well, how to indicate a relationship is not going well, or is over, and how to express **regret**
- life in general – metaphors used when life is going well, metaphors used to indicate life is not going well, metaphors which comment on the nature of life itself.

Talking about people's personalities

Language practice

What do you mean by that?
I've never heard that expression before.
Do you mean ...?
What did you say about him/her?
That's a strange expression.
Oh, I see. You mean ...?

Real-life conversation

Scene: A husband and wife, Nikolai and Katrina are being driven home by their friend, Neil, from a party

Neil: What did you think of Michael's wife?

	She's a bit of a mouse, isn't she?
Nikolai:	A mouse? What do you mean by that?
Neil:	Well, she's very timid, wouldn't say boo to a goose.
Katrina:	She was very quiet compared to her husband.
Neil:	That's not difficult. Mike is a party animal.
Nikolai:	I've never heard that expression before.
Katrina:	Do you mean he behaves like an animal? I thought he was charming.
Neil:	No. I mean he's very sociable. He likes company. **Apparently** his wife's very academic. He calls her a **bookworm**.
Nikolai:	Katrina reads a lot too. She likes Russian **literature,** don't you, Katrina?
Katrina:	Yes, we had a long conversation about Tolstoy. She had just read Anna Karenina.
Nikolai:	Michael's wife looked tired.
Neil:	You're right there, dog-tired.
Katrina:	She'd been up early this morning preparing food.
Neil:	Poor her. She won't have got much support from Mike. He's always weaselling out of things.
Neil:	Weaselling out?
Nikolai:	Avoiding things. He's like that at work. If he doesn't want to do something he'll make an excuse not too.
Katrina:	I understand your explanation, but what is a weasel?
Neil:	A tiny little animal. It's very long and thin, so it can easily get away from danger. I reckon Mike's got a few hours to go yet. He's an owl, is Mike.
Nikolai:	What did you say about him?
Neil:	He's an owl?

Nikolai:	Oh, I see. You mean he likes to be up at night.
Katrina:	I'm tired too. I'm at my best in the morning.
Neil:	So you're up with the larks.
Maria:	That's a strange expression.
Nikolai:	I hope you're not saying my wife is crazy.
Neil:	No, of course not. A lark gets up early. It's a cuckoo that means a crazy person.

Talking about work relationships

Language practice

I'm sorry. I'm still not sure what you mean.
What do you mean?
You'd like me to...
Do you mean...?
I understand now you've explained it.
Is that the correct expression?

Real-life conversation

*Scene: a busy office at nine in the morning. Shobna is talking to her **assistant**, Mia*

Shobna:	I've got to go out this morning, Mia, so I'm leaving you to hold the fort.
Mia:	I'm sorry. I don't understand.
Shobna:	Hold the fort. I mean keep an eye on things, make sure everything runs smoothly.
Mia:	I'm sorry. I'm still not sure what you mean.
Shobna:	I'm going out, so you will be in **charge** of the office.
Mia:	Ah. I understand now. How long will you be gone?

Shobna:	I'm not sure. I have an appointment with the bank manager. He said we're in the red.
Mia:	In the red?
Shobna:	It's just an expression. He says we have no money in the bank. We've spent too much.
Mia:	Do you mean the company has an overdraft?
Shobna:	Yes. I'm sure he's making a mountain out of a **molehill**, but I'd better go.
Mia:	What do you mean? I don't understand what you said about mountains.
Shobna:	Sorry. I'm sure it's just a little problem, not a big problem. I'm not sure how long I'll be.
Mia:	Thank you. I understand now you've explained it.
Shobna:	Can you phone and report the fault in the **photocopier**. I'm sure they've sold us a lemon.
Mia:	I will phone about the broken photocopier. You'd like me to buy a lemon?
Shobna:	No! No! I said I think they sold us a lemon. When a machine breaks down soon after it's been bought, we call it a lemon. Can you phone Mr. Jones and apologise about the mistake we made with his order. I'm sure he asked for 5, but now he's got them he says he ordered ten boxes. The customer is king.
Mia:	Mr. Jones is king? King of where?
Shobna:	He's not king of anywhere. It's just an expression. The customer is king means that the customer is always right. If we want to keep our customers we must do as they ask.

Mia:	Of course. If Mr. Jones is not happy, he will use another company.
Shobna:	You're right there, Mia. In the world of business it's dog eat dog. You have to be strong to survive.
Mia:	You'd like me to hold the fort. Is that the correct expression?
Shobna:	That's right. You take charge here and I'll face the music. That means I'll see what the bank manager has to say, good or bad.

Talking about personal relationships

Language practice

Do you mean to say that...?
What are you trying to tell me?
Do I understand you correctly?
And what makes you think that?

Real-life situation

Scene: Rita arrives at the house of her friend Inez

Inez:	Thank you so much for coming.
Rita:	I got your phone call. You sounded upset. Is something wrong?
Inez:	Yes. I think my relationship with Peter is on the rocks.
Rita:	I'm not sure what you mean, Inez.
Inez:	Peter came to see me last night and he said we're at a **crossroads**.
Rita:	What do you mean exactly? At a crossroads.
Inez:	It's a metaphor, a figure of speech. It means we are past the point of no return.
Rita:	Is that a figure of speech too?

Inez:	Yes, I suppose it is.
Rita:	What are you trying to tell me?
Inez:	Well, I think he's saying that he wants to end our relationship.
Rita:	I can't believe that, you are perfect for each other.
Inez:	That's what I thought. We've come so far in the last few months. Julie did say he was too old for me, though – maybe she was right.
Rita:	That was just sour grapes.
Inez:	What do you mean, sour grapes?
Rita:	I mean she said that because she was jealous. Her marriage is on the rocks.
Inez:	Do I understand you correctly? Are you saying their marriage is over?
Rita:	Not over exactly, but they are having problems.
Inez:	I thought all was blue skies there. They seem so happy.
Rita:	No, it's been a long, bumpy road. They are expert at hiding their problems from other people.
Inez:	So they're having problems too. Is she still angry about that **incident** at work?
Rita:	Yes. I told her she should let sleeping dogs lie.
Inez:	What does that mean?
Rita:	That you shouldn't keep arguing about things that happened in the past.
Inez:	I see. You mean she should forget about it. The past can't cause trouble unless you allow it to.
Rita:	Exactly. I'm sure you're mistaken about Peter, by the way.
Inez:	And what makes you think that?

Rita:	I probably shouldn't be telling you this, but he told John he was planning to **propose** to you.
Inez:	Never!
Rita:	He did. He was asking his advice about it.
Inez:	Do you think that was what he was trying to say when he said we were at a crossroads?
Rita:	Yes, you idiot. He was probably trying **to lead up to** a proposal.
Inez:	I don't believe it. I've been chewing over his words all day, thinking about what he said over and over again.
Rita:	Well stop chewing and **give him a call**.

Talking about your life

Language practice

I've never heard that before.
I guess it means ...
Am I right?
I'm not sure I know what you mean.
You didn't mean that literally, did you?

Real-life conversation

Scene: Richard meets Ben at the bus stop

Richard:	You're looking smart, Ben. Where are you going?
Ben:	I've got an interview for a job at the college.
Richard:	That's great.
Ben:	I'm so nervous. Jobs like this come up once in a blue moon.
Richard:	Once in a blue moon, I've never heard that before. I guess it means not very often. It's a rare opportunity. Am I right?

Ben:	Yes.
Richard:	There's going to be a **panel** of five people interviewing me. I think I've bitten off more than I can chew.
Ben:	Do you mean you think that's more than you can handle? You don't feel confident about this interview?
Richard:	**You can say that again.**
Ben:	Just remember that in an interview you have to take the **reins**.
Richard:	I'm not sure I know what you mean.
Ben:	Keep in **control**. Don't let them **pressure** you.
Richard:	Thanks, mate. I'll remember that. Didn't you have an interview yourself last week?
Ben:	Yes, but I didn't get the job. You know, you win some, you lose some.
Richard:	Yes, life is a game, isn't it?
Ben:	It's been a ride for me lately.
Richard:	What do you mean?
Ben:	Well, I've had lots of ups and downs, like a **roller coaster**. I was really disappointed when I didn't get that job. Then I heard the man who had got it worked at the factory across the road from my house. I phoned them up, went for an interview for the job he was leaving, and I start next week. They said he'd only left because he was moving to the other side of the city.
Richard:	That was clever of you.
Ben:	When life throws you lemons, make lemonade. That's my **motto**.
Richard:	You didn't mean that **literally**, did you? I'm starting **to get the hang of** these metaphors. You know I feel much more confident now.

Ben: You go in there and do your best, Richard. Remember, in the game of life, there's no **reset button.**

Richard: No reset button?

Ben: It's another metaphor. You only live once, so make the most of it.

Language transfer

What did you think of ...?

(What's your opinion of ...?)
What did you think of Michael's wife?
What did you think of the film/play/game etc.?
What did you think of the news?

To get the hang of (to become used to, to be able to do or say)

I'm getting the hang of these metaphors.
Keep practising, you'll soon get the hang of it.
I can't get the hang of this. Could you help/show me.

To lead up to (to do something in preparation for something else)

He was leading up to a proposal.
There are lots of small events leading up to one big one.

Helping you learn

Progress questions

1 How many ways can you find of asking someone to explain a metaphor or expression you don't understand?

2 Can you find metaphors which have the opposite meaning, for example, an owl and a lark?

Discussion points

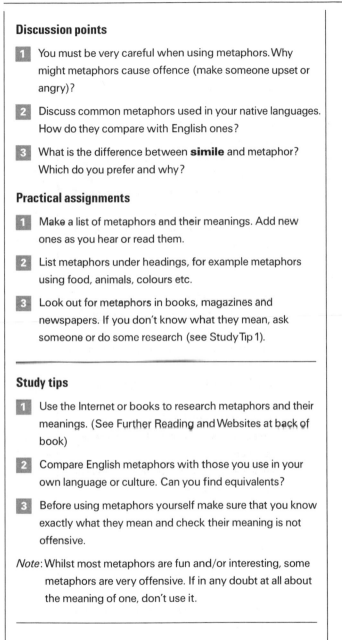

1 You must be very careful when using metaphors. Why might metaphors cause offence (make someone upset or angry)?

2 Discuss common metaphors used in your native languages. How do they compare with English ones?

3 What is the difference between **simile** and metaphor? Which do you prefer and why?

Practical assignments

1 Make a list of metaphors and their meanings. Add new ones as you hear or read them.

2 List metaphors under headings, for example metaphors using food, animals, colours etc.

3 Look out for metaphors in books, magazines and newspapers. If you don't know what they mean, ask someone or do some research (see Study Tip 1).

Study tips

1 Use the Internet or books to research metaphors and their meanings. (See Further Reading and Websites at back of book)

2 Compare English metaphors with those you use in your own language or culture. Can you find equivalents?

3 Before using metaphors yourself make sure that you know exactly what they mean and check their meaning is not offensive.

Note: Whilst most metaphors are fun and/or interesting, some metaphors are very offensive. If in any doubt at all about the meaning of one, don't use it.

Glossary

assistant	a person who helps or assists another person
academic	a person who likes to study or learn
apparently	people say that, it is known that
bookworm	someone who is often reading
charge	to take charge: to be in control
colleague	someone with whom you work
control	to guide, be in charge, order
crossroads	literally, a junction, place where two roads cross
customer	a person who buys things from a shop or company
expression	a saying, something which
incident	an event, something which happens
literally	truly, really, exactly
literature	books, often from a particular place or culture
metaphor	comparing two things by saying one thing is another
molehill	a pile of earth made by a mole, a small underground animal
motto	a short saying, proverb or mantra
panel	a group of people chosen to interview or question
photocopier	an office machine which takes a paper copy
pressure	when someone feels they must act or decide quickly
propose	to ask someone to do something, here to marry you
reckon	to think or guess
regret	to wish you hadn't done something
reins	long straps used to guide a horse
reset button	a button on a machine which allows you to undo something
roller coaster	a fairground ride with a fast curved track; a big dipper

simile	comparing two things using like or as ie., as white as snow, he's like a ghost

Colloquial phrases

he/she is a bit of ...	She is a bit of a mouse.

> *Note*: This is a deliberate under-statement meaning she is *very* similar to a mouse.

He's a bit silly.	He's very silly.
He/she's a bit of all right.	He or she's very attractive.
give him a call/text	telephone/text him
You can say that again.	You don't feel confident about this interview.
	You can say that again. (You're right about that.)
	This means he actually feels very unconfident.
	You don't like eggs.
	You can say that again. (Actually I hate eggs.)

Appendix
Numbers and
Dates

Numbers

Cardinal numbers

0	nought, zero, nothing	19	nineteen
1	one	20	twenty
2	two	21	twenty-one
3	three	30	thirty
4	four	40	forty
6	six	50	fifty
7	seven	60	sixty
8	eight	70	seventy
9	nine	80	eighty
10	ten	90	ninety
11	eleven	100	a/one hundred
12	twelve	500	five hundred
13	thirteen	167	a hundred and sixty-seven
14	fourteen	1,000	one thousand
15	fifteen	1,000,000	one million
16	sixteen		
17	seventeen	*Note*: commas are not
18	eighteen	always used.

Ordinal numbers

1st	first	9th	ninth
2nd	second	10th	tenth
3rd	third	20th	twentieth
4th	fourth	21st	twenty-first
5th	fifth	23rd	twenty-third
6th	sixth	30th	thirtieth
7th	seventh	100th	a/one hundredth
8th	eighth		

Dates

Days of the week
Monday
Tuesday
Wednesday
Thursday
Friday
Saturday
Sunday

Months of the year
January
February
March
April
May
June
July
August
September
October
November
December

Further Reading

Spoken English

Activate Your English. Barbara Sinclair and Philip Prowse
(Cambridge University Press).
Cambridge First Certificate: Listening and Speaking.
(Cambridge University Press).
Elementary Task Listening. Jacqueline St Clair Stokes
(Cambridge University Press).
Essential telephoning in English Students/Teachers Books.
Barbara Garside and Tony Garside. (Cambridge
University Press).
*Keep Talking: Communicative Fluency Activities for Language
Teaching.* (Cambridge University Press).
Phrases. Hugh & Margaret Brown (Brown and Brown).
Pronunciation Tasks: A Course for Pre-intermediate Learners.
Martin Hewings (Cambridge University Press).
Simple Speaking Activities. Jill Hadfield, Charles Hadfield
(Oxford Basics).

Vocabulary

Advanced Vocabulary and Idiom. B. J. Thomas (Longman).
Build Your Vocabulary (set of three). John Flower &
Michael Berman (Language Teaching Publications).
Elementary Vocabulary. B. J. Thomas (Longman).
*English Vocabulary in Use: Pre-intermediate and
Intermediate.* Stuart Redman (Cambridge University
Press).
Intermediate Vocabulary. B. J. Thomas (Longman).
Start Building Your Vocabulary. John Flower (Language
Teaching Publications).
Vocabulary in Practice (set). Glennis Pye (Cambridge
University Press).

Dictionaries

Active Study Dictionary. (Longman).

Cobuild English Dictionary. John Sinclair (Harper Collins).
Cobuild Dictionary of Phrasal Verbs. John Sinclair (Harper Collins).
Oxford Elementary Learners' Dictionary. (Oxford University Press).
Oxford English Picture Dictionary. E. C. Parnwell (Oxford University Press; also Dual Language Editions).
Oxford Photo Dictionary. (Oxford University Press).
Photo Dictionary. Marilyn S. Rosenthal & Daniel B. Freeman (Longman).
Today's English Dictionary. John Sinclair (Harper Collins).

Grammar

Cambridge First Certificate Grammar and Usage. Bob Obee (Cambridge University Press).
Cobuild Elementary English Grammar. (Harper Collins).
Cobuild English Guides 7: Metaphor. (Harper Collins).
Cobuild Student's Grammar. Dave Willis (Harper Collins).
English Grammar in Use: A Self-study Reference and Practice Book. Raymond Murphy (Cambridge University Press).
English Grammar in Use: Supplementary Exercises. Louise Hashemi with Raymond Murphy (Cambridge University Press).
Essential Grammar in Use: A Self-study Reference and Practice Book. Raymond Murphy (Cambridge University Press).
Essential Grammar in Use: Supplementary Exercises. Helen Naylor with Raymond Murphy (Cambridge University Press).
First English Grammar. Celia Blisset & Katherine Hallgarten (Language Teaching Publications).
Grammar in Practice. Jimmie Hill & Rosalyn Hurst.
Grammar in Practice. (set) Roger Gower (Cambridge).
Teach Yourself Correct English. B. A. Phythion (Hodder & Stoughton).

Jobseeking

An A-Z of Careers and Jobs. Diane Burston (Kogan Page).
On the Job English. Christy M. Newman (New Reader's Press).
Practise Your CV Writing. Christine Baker (Avanti Books).
Preparing Your Own CV. Rebecca Corfield (Kogan Page).
Successful Interview Skills. Rebecca Corfield (Kogan Page).
Writing Away for a Job. Sally McKeown (BEN Unit).

Telephone skills

Basic telephone Training. Anne Watson-Delestree (Language Teaching Publications).
How to use a Telephone Directory (worksheets) (The Printed Resources Unit).

Mail Order

Using Mail Order Catalogues. Linda Storey & Bridget Coates (The Printed Resources Unit).

ESOL Resources

A Tutor's Guide to ESOL Materials for Adult Learners. Helen Sutherland (Language and Literacy Unit).

Course books

Help Yourself to English. Robert Leach, Elizabeth Knight, John Johnson (National Extension College).

Note – All the books listed can be ordered from Avanti Books, 8 Parsons Green, Boulton Road, Stevenage, Hertfordshire SG1 4QG.

Useful Addresses

Examination Boards

City & Guilds of London Institute, 1 Giltspur Street, London EC1A 9DD. Tel: 020 7294 2468

Royal Society of Arts Examinations, Progress House, Westwood Way, Coventry CV4 8HS. Tel: 024 7647 0033

Associations for language teaching

Association for Language Learning, 150 Railway Terrace, Rugby, Warwickshire CV21 3HN. Tel: 01788 546443

Centre for Information on Language Teaching and Research, 20 Bedfordbury, Covent Garden, London WC2N 4LB. Tel: 020 7379 5101

International Language Centres Group, International House White Rock, Hastings, East Sussex TN34 1JY. Tel: +44 1424 720100

National Association for the Teaching of English (NATE), 50 Broadfield Road, Broadfield Business Centre, Sheffield S8 0XS. Tel: 0114 225 5419

National Association for Teaching English and other Community Languages to Adults (NATECLA), National Centre, South Birmingham College, 524 Stratford Road, Birmingham B11 4AJ. Tel: 0121 694 5071

Book publishers

Avanti Books, 8 Parsons Green, Boulton Road, Stevenage, Herts SG1 4QG. Tel: 01438 350155, 745876, 745877

Cambridge University Press, Publishing Division, The Edinburgh Building, Cambridge CB2 2RU

Oxford University Press, Walton Street, Oxford OX2 6DP

Other organisations

BBC Education Information Unit, White City, 201 Wood Lane, London W12 7TS. Tel: 020 8746 1111

Department of Social Security, Pensions and Overseas Benefits Directorate, JBES, Room TC001, Tyneview Park, Whitely Road, Benton, Newcastle-upon-Tyne NE98 1BA

DVLA (Driver and Vehicle Licensing Agency), Swansea SA99 1AJ

Post Office Users National Council, 6 Hercules Road, London SE1 7DN. Tel: 020 7928 9458

Royal Mail Direct, British Philatelic Bureau, Freepost, SC0 2250, 20 Brandon St, Edinburgh EH3 0BR

Websites

Disclaimer

The internet, or world wide web, is a wonderful resource. It will give you nearly free and almost immediate information on any topic. Ignore this vast and valuable store of materials at your peril! To find current web sites that are useful to students learning to speak English, please log on to www.studymates.co.uk and then click on the link to the Speaking English page.

Please note that neither the author nor the publisher is responsible for content or opinions expressed on the sites listed, which are simply intended to offer starting points for students. Also, please remember that the internet is a fast-changing environment, and links may come and go.

If you have some favourite sites you would like to see listed, please write to Dorothy Massey, c/o Studymates (address on back cover). You can also email her at:

dorothymassey@studymates.co.uk

Happy surfing!

UK Study Contact Details

UKStudy.com Ltd, Enterprise House, 83a Western Road, Hove, East Sussex BN3 1JB, England. Tel: (+44) (0)1273 72 55 77. Fax: (+44) (0)1273 72 44 66
Email: info@ukstudy.com

Europa Pages

www.europa-pages.com/uk/index.

English Language Schools

There are hundreds to choose from, we have listed some at www.studymates.co.uk and will happily extend the list by adding new names.

Telephoning and/or faxing Britain

To telephone or fax Britain from abroad, dial your international access code, followed by 44 and the full phone number minus the first 0. eg: 020 7213 472 becomes +44 20 7213 472

Au Pair Work

- *Note:* Due to government regulations, Britain only accepts au pairs from certain countries: Andorra, Austria, Belgium, Boznia-Herzegovina, Bulgaria, Croatia, Cyprus, Czech Republic, Denmark, Estonia, Finland, France, Germany, Greece, Greenland, Hungary, Iceland, Ireland, Italy, Latvia, Liechtenstein, Lithuania, Luxembourg, Macedonia, Malta, Monaco, Norway, Poland, Portugal, Romania, San Marino, Slovak Republic, Slovenia, Spain, Sweden, Switzerland, The Faroes, The Netherlands, Turkey.

Contact: Elaine Dickens, Woodfalls Lodge, Loxwood Road, Rudgwick, West Sussex RH12 3DW, UNITED KINGDOM. Tel: 00 44 (0)1403 824217. Fax: 00 44 (0)1403 823014 Email: elaine@e-aupairs.com Web: www.e-aupairs.com

Contact: Maggie Dyer, The London Au Pair & Nanny Agency, 4 Sunnyside, Childs Hill, London. NW2 2QN, UNITED KINGDOM. Tel: +44 20 7435 3891. Fax: +44 20 7794 2700
Email: info@londonaupair.co.uk
Web: www.londonaupair.co.uk

Contact: Alena Udovic-Korutaro, 42 Belgrave Rd, Margate, Kent, CT9 1XG, UNITED KINGDOM. Tel: UK FREEPHONE: 0800 096 4916/00 44 (0) 1843 571 716. Fax: 00 44 (0)1843 22 88 60
Email: info@a1kidscare.co.uk   Web: www.a1kidscare.com

Contact: Vivienne Colchester, 42 Underhill Road, London SE22 0QT, UNITED KINGDOM. Tel: +44 (0)20 8299 3052. Fax: +44 (0)20 8299 6086.
Email: vivienne@abc-aupairs.co.uk
Web: www.abc-aupairs.co.uk

Contact: Damian Kirkwood, 4 Napier Road, Holland Park, London W14 8LQ, UNITED KINGDOM. Tel: +44 (0)1288 359 159. Fax: +44 (0)1288 359 159
Email: Admin@aupair-agency.com
Web: www.aupair-agency.com and www.nanny-agency.com

There are more au-pair agencies in the UK, for more details visit www.europa-pages.com/cgi-bin/aupair/agency.cgi

Tourist Information

England
For details of the British Monarchy, including visiting times to the State Rooms at Buckingham, visit www.royal.gov.uk

For details of the historic Royal Palaces: www.hrp.org.uk

For travel details visit www.travelbritain.com

Wales

Experience the part of Britain where another language other than English is spoken. In North Wales you will hear Welsh being spoken in normal everyday life. For more details visit www.nwt.co.uk/english/coastal/fs.htm Studymates, the publishers of this book, are now based in North Wales.

Do not miss out on the exquisite beauty of Snowdonia. For more details contact North Wales Tourism, 77 Conwy Road, Colwyn Bay, LL29 7LN. Tel: 01492 531731.
Fax: 01492 530059
Email: croeso@nwt.co.uk (Croeso is Welsh for welcome.)

Scotland

If you are visiting the UK in the Summer, you will have the opportunity to visit the Edinburgh festival, a cultural festival o for the whole of the UK. For more information see www.edinburgh.org/

Ireland

It is possible to combine a visit to the UK with a visit to our neighbours in Ireland. For details of festivals and places to see, visit www.tourismireland.com or www.tourist-information-dublin.co.uk

London Underground

For relevant information, visit www.tube.tfl.gov.uk/content/faq/tourism/introduction.asp

Visas for the UK

To visit the UK you *must* have a visa. You will still then need to pass through immigration control. For more information see www.britain.or.ug/visa_info/visitors.htm

HM Customs and Excise

For details on what you can bring into the UK without being charged duty, visit www.hmce.gov.uk

Health matters

For health matters visit www.publications.doh.gov.uk/ overseasvisitors/study1

You can obtain advice about a health problem 24 hours a day from NHS Direct, tel: 0845 46 47 or via the web on www.nhsdirect.nhs.uk

Driving in the UK

See www.thinkroadsafety.gov.uk/advice/keepleft

Emergency

In an emergency call 999 from any UK phone box. The call is free and help will be given. When you hear the voice of the operator ask for Police, Fire or Ambulance. For an emergency at sea you still call 999 and ask for the Coastguard. Explain that you are a visitor and that you are learning English. Talk clearly and give as much clear information as possible, then the emergency services will be able to help you.

Index